Adult Learning in Groups

Adult Learning in Groups

Bríd Connolly

 Open University Press

Open University Press
McGraw-Hill Education
McGraw-Hill House
Shoppenhangers Road
Maidenhead
Berkshire
England
SL6 2QL

email: enquiries@openup.co.uk
world wide web: www.openup.co.uk

and Two Penn Plaza, New York, NY 10121-2289, USA

First published 2008

A catalogue record of this book is available from the British Library

ISBN-13: 978-0-33-522860-7 (pb)   978-0-33-522859-1 (hb)
ISBN-10: 033522860-7 (pb)   033522859-3 (hb)

Library of Congress Cataloging-in-Publication Data
CIP data applied for

Fictitious names of companies, products, people, characters and/or data that may be used herein (in case studies or in examples) are not intended to represent any real individual, company, product or event

Typeset by BookEns Ltd, Royston, Herts.
Printed in the UK by Bell and Bain Ltd, Glasgow.

The **McGraw-Hill** Companies

Contents

Acknowledgements

I want to thank Con Delaney, Aogán Delaney and Eavan Connolly for all their support and encouragement, throughout the process of writing this book. Thanks also to my extended family. Sincere thanks to Anne B. Ryan and David McCormack, and to all my colleagues in the Department of Adult and Community Education, NUIM and the wider adult and community education arena. I am also very grateful to people who have commented on the work. Finally, I owe an incalculable debt to the people with whom I worked in learning groups throughout the years. Thank you.

1 Roadmap of *Adult Learning in Groups*

Key ideas: adult education; community education; lifelong learning; the role in civil society; adult learners; adult learning; reflective practice; social transformation

Introduction

If there is a common bond that links all adult learners, it is around some idea of improvement, development, enhancement or advancement. Adult learning is about attaining new knowledge, of course, but that process is about new perspectives, too: changing ourselves in some way. As we set out on the learning journey, we are in a state of flux: we will never be the same again. We aspire towards a being a better self, developing our potential, challenging ourselves. If we consider the stages of development that mark the early years of our lives, from communicating with our parents to playing with friends, we perceive these as essential to our being. Adult learning is of the same order: it helps us to become the person we can be. But adult learning is more than the incremental stages of personal development. Developing our potential is a commitment to become more fully human. Becoming more human includes the adult concern with our attitudes, values and beliefs, in addition to learning more, getting qualifications and developing new skills. Newly developed knowledge challenges our foundational values and beliefs. New knowledge illuminates old knowledge. A brief review of human history shows that – in spite of huge retrogressive leaps through war, conflict, the abuse of power – we are trying to make the world a better place to live in. We are outraged at injustice. We have created and we support institutions that attempt to redress injustice, such as the legal system and the educational system. Democracy, though imperfect, is an example of the desire to create a system that draws on human intelligences and ethical codes to replace blind obedience to an authoritarian leader. So also are the freedoms that are commonplace in the modern world, including the freedom to think for ourselves, freedom to be different, freedom of belief, underpinned by the system of rights in the UN Declaration of Human Rights. And we all share in the benefits of these rights. Thus, being an adult learner links us to the huge process of human, community and social development, even if we play just a tiny role in the overall endeavour.

This book is about adults learning in groups. I want to explore the implications of learning in groups in order to shed light on the processes involved, to enhance our understanding of these processes and to enable us to use them for the benefit of learners. The book is for adult educators, and it will provide them with a resource for their practice. It is also for adult learners, to help them to reflect on the experience of learning. This chapter will explore the dimensions of adult education in the wider context of lifelong learning, and will look at what it means to be an adult educator in that environment. This environment is fluid and variable, and being an adult educator is demanding in terms of the role in the knowledge society as well as the role in terms of meeting learners' needs. I will also consider also the learners participating in adult learning, and look at the how groupwork in learning groups has developed as a distinct area due to the accumulated evaluation from these learners. First, this chapter will outline the entire volume, in order to contextualize what I mean by adults learning in groups: what groups, what learners and what adult educators.

The book

If you are looking to this book for techniques to keep people quiet while you teach, or to encourage them to accept your authority without question, then this is probably not the book for you. However, it may help you to think about why this is your approach. I have based this book on my experience of working with adults in learning groups for over twenty years, as an adult and community educator. In addition, I have also used my experience as a learner. During those twenty-odd years, I studied in order to develop my own professional capacity, and of course, to ensure that I didn't settle for doing the same old things. I learned not just from the content of the courses, but also from the processes. Indeed, I learned a lot about what *not* to do, with many lecturers and tutors completely incapable of democracy and equality, not recognizing that they were working with adults. My deepest learning, though, came from the learners in the groups I facilitated or tutored, and my fellow learners. Most especially, I learned that people respond to respect, tolerance and consideration, and these are probably the most important qualities for adult educators to have. Of course, this does *not* mean that learners will passively accept what the educators want them to accept. So, if this is one of your motivations for studying groupwork for adult learning, then I must warn you, that this book will not answer your need. This book is about enabling learners to become more active, more self-motivated, more capable of reflecting critically. That is, it is about enabling learners to challenge the way things are in order to bring about their own development as well as a more widespread human and social development. This book aims to do the opposite of what we think of a 'group mentality', an unquestioning acceptance of the diktats of the group leader, whether the leader is the teacher, community worker, public representative, or whatever. The outcomes include empowering learners to challenge passivity and to develop their capacity to think for themselves.

Incidentally, this book aims to elucidate the processes involved in these contexts, in order to make the most of them for co-learners and facilitators. It is therefore useful not just for the professionals in formal adult education, but also for those working with adults in many circumstances, like shop assistants, people involved in community work and active citizenship, complementary health advocates, team leaders, and so on, in the landscape of adult education.

Next I will broadly describe the terms and areas that are involved when we speak about adults learning in groups. I will consider the meanings of adult education, community education, adult educators, facilitation, groupwork, reflective practice and related areas. Then I will discuss how you can use this book in your own work. Finally, I will look at the organization of the book, outlining and contextualizing the contents of each chapter, and providing the thread that links these separate sections. The next section will look at adult education in all its myriad forms.

Adult education

When we speak about school or college, we have a good idea about what happens in these environments. If we picture them in our inner eye, they take the format based on our own experience. However, it is not as easy to picture adult education. In my experience of learning as an adult, I have been in learning environments that were both usual and completely unexpected and delightful. I have sat in rooms with rows of tables and chairs or fixed desks, and in lecture theatres. I have shivered in community halls with plastic stacking chairs gathered around a tiny heater. I doodled in hotel rooms around large conference tables. I perched in front of technical consoles, concentrating on *not* pushing the wrong button. I ambled around a multi-skills training room, trying my hand at different crafts and arts, and followed expert guides around cities, exhibition spaces and museums. I puzzled in front of computers, ready to howl with frustration, and listened to tapes, trying to guess the meanings of the impenetrable new languages. Most memorably, for one course, I sat enchanted on a lawn, in glorious summer shade. All of these environments, together with many others, are adult learning environments. Sometimes we do not see ourselves as learners yet we acquire so much new knowledge and skills in these contexts. Just think about technological advances since the 1980s, and the enthusiasm with which the population at large meets these advances. New ways of communicating have transformed our social lives, from what we called long-distance telephone calls, to emailing and texting. If we did not learn, we would be unable to acquire new skills to improve and progress in our work. We would not able to travel to new places. Our leisure time, from hobbies to keeping fit, all depend on learning new information about our pursuits in order to make the most of them. The major life events like pregnancy and marriage have attendant education courses attached to them, which help to alleviate our anxieties. Health authorities and agencies have a wide range of adult education, from training in reflexology to using a hearing aid; from nutrition to the Alexander Technique. Human rights organizations rely on conferences, articles, testimonies, news-sheets and so on, to provide information to activists. In all aspects of our lives, learning plays a pivotal role in our participation in and enjoyment of the community and our personal lives. Indeed, adult education is a leisure activity for many people, and groups attend all kinds of classes that brighten their dark winter nights. When we speak of adult education, this is what we are talking about. Adult education includes all education that adults undertake, after they are finished with their compulsory education provision.

Adult education falls into four categories, with some overlap (Foley, 2004: 4–5). The ubiquitous adult learning is that of *incidental adult education*. When we struggle to understand the technical aspects of new equipment, like a DVD player or mobile phone, incidental adult education occurs. Examples include finding our way around a new city, listening to gardening programmes, browsing the internet or encyclopaedias, journaling. Incidental adult education is almost an unintentional outcome of an activity. In many ways, incidental adult education is not even seen as learning. Rather, it is put down to experience, or seen as an inevitable part of living. My experience of incidental adult education includes using my digital camera or discovering new facets to a city as I find my way around it.

Formal adult education consists of programmes for adults, run by professional adult educators and providers, which culminate in awards such as certificates, diplomas and degrees, and in qualifications. It includes vocational training, university courses, further education, and so on. In my own experience, my formal adult education took place in university when I qualified as an adult educator.

The third category is the *non-formal* one. This includes all adult education without qualifications. The courses in the non-formal provision include leisure type courses, such as painting or creative writing; citizenship education, such as estate management, or political activism; and, probably the best known, adult literacy education. My experience in the non-formal arena involved a range of courses, from a community drama one-off workshop to a twelve-session series in arts and crafts. Non-formal adult education is organized and usually involves a trained tutor, not necessarily paid, as voluntary tutors have been the backbone of this sector. However, some tutors come from the community. For example, married couples may lead a pre-marriage programme, or an actor may direct a voice workshop, drawing on their own experiences.

The fourth category, *informal adult education* is not necessarily organized by adult education organizers, nor do they necessarily have a facilitator or a curriculum. Informal adult education includes the type of education that takes place in consciousness-raising groups, like women's groups and disability groups. It occurs in film and book clubs, when people discuss their response to the film or book. It transpires when groups of people take time to think about what they are doing. These groups can include community groups, work teams and sports clubs.

Therefore, when we are speaking about adult education, we are speaking about a wide range of learning environments together with an array of co-learners and facilitators.

Community education

Community education is difficult to define, but this does not inhibit its success. In Ireland it has a particular history which is quite different to the UK, even when the same term is used. But the Irish model is useful to look at in terms of the possibilities for community education, and perhaps inspiring for adults wishing to take possession of a process that exemplifies community activism that empowers people in a fundamental way.

The White Paper in Adult Education, *Learning for Life* (Government of Ireland, 2000) sees it as currently the most dynamic, creative and relevant aspect of education with adults in Ireland. It maintains that it has a multitude of characteristics including rootedness in the community; being based on process rather than syllabus; promoting social and collective outcomes, including critical reflection and empowerment; promoting participative democracy; and having a concern for congruence between the content and process of adult learning with the needs of the learners and the community (pp. 112–13). Community education thrives among self-directed community activists, and it succeeds because it is *of* the community and *for* the community. It opens the doors to learning that probably had been closed in mainstream education, and these doors lead to subjects that are awe inspiring, meaningful to people's lives and pleasurable. Its strength lies especially in its capacity to reach very vulnerable people, people who may not engage with civil society except, perhaps, in terms of social welfare. Many of these people have been failed by formal schooling, the health service and the political system, and as such, find it difficult to have their voices heard. Community education has responded to the lived experiences of people and has engaged with participants to come up with learning programmes that meet their needs. In Ireland, the women's community education movement has touched women's lives in ways that other social movements failed to. Indeed, women's community education has enabled women to become activists in ways that really suit them, in terms of not only organizing and maintaining community education programmes and projects, but also exceeding the statutory providers when it comes to the development of adult education methods and programmes. Crucially, the slogan of the founders and pioneers was '*no classes without crèches*', and the statutory providers have failed to come near this, in Ireland at least.

It is telling to look at the women's community education movement in Ireland as a model that has lessons for the entire arena of community education. Women's community education emerged in Ireland in the early 1980s, and, within a few years, had spread all over the island. It was rooted in the community at a very difficult time in Ireland. There was a high level of unemployment, emigration and poverty at the time; the war in Northern Ireland was truly terrible; and the news brought first-hand images of the horror of the famine in Ethiopia. The decade had started off quite well, just as we were moving towards a more secular society, especially with the help of the European Union. With these factors as a background, among so many others, of course, women started organizing classes for themselves, particularly women who worked in the home. Reflecting on women's community education on the twentieth anniversary of my involvement, I noted that it was markedly different to the adult education that the statutory agencies and universities offered beforehand, and that it had characteristics that fortified the movement that ensued. These characteristics include ownership, agency, subjectivity and consciousness raising (Connolly, 2005: 206–7). The programmes belong to the women who organize them and the participants within them. The organizers have the power to choose facilitators and courses. They reach out to new participants, welcoming them into the learning environment, and helping them to identify their needs from the programme. The provision goes well beyond a set number of hours of tuition. It includes setting up the space, taking part in classes and organizing committees, listening to other participants and conducting overall evaluations. This kind of reflexivity signals the notion of agency, which entails a self-sufficiency, autonomy and self-direction, ensuring that the programmes meet their learning needs, social and personal. Women's community education analyses social and personal experience, locating it in the subjective knowledge, before moving into knowledge that is relatively more objective. That is, it does not privilege objectivity over subjectivity. This overturns traditional education fundamentally, and while this is not unique to women's community education, it has had the effect of introducing it to other educational fora. Further, women's community education fosters consciousness raising, a process forged in the women's movement and popular education, particularly in what is termed *critical adult education* which is considered in greater detail in Chapter 4. Consciousness raising is the process of looking at familiar life experiences and interpreting these in social and cultural terms, rather than individualistic or private ones. For example, a woman in community education may endure a difficult issue such as domestic violence. With consciousness raising, this is analysed as a criminal assault, a crime against the victim and society, rather than a private, shameful issue within the family. This may seem obvious, but for many victims of domestic violence, this perspective is revolutionary, in spite of the prevalence of support agencies. For a woman in community education, the learning environment enables her to look at her painful situation, developing the consciousness that her situation is not her own fault, nor a private matter. The wider access to knowledge and dialogue helps her to see it in a much wider context, even if she does not speak about it. And one of the key features of women's community education is the message that permeates the atmosphere, that any one woman is not on her own, that there are others there who are supportive and nurturing. Thus, women's community education is a unique set of characteristics, which together provide a model for all other community education programmes.

A certain ambiguity surrounds community education. Women's community education is not simply adult education offered in the community; it responds to community needs, and it depends on community effort. People who do not understand this reduce it to a concept of community-based education, which extends to 'hard-to-reach' populations. Yet community education has the capacity to enhance participative democracy, and to engage otherwise alienated people in civil society.

Adult and community education has a wider context in non-traditional education: that of lifelong learning. The next section will look at the emergence of lifelong learning, and its attendant companions of lifewide learning and lifedeep learning, to help to clarify them and to locate adult education within the thinking around them.

Lifelong learning

Lifelong learning has myriad definitions but all contain the essential elements of educational and learning opportunities for people through-out their lifetimes (Tight, 2002: 39), from the incidental childhood learning of walking and talking, to the non-formal class in yoga and painting of the senior citizen clubs. The European community is concerned with democracy, social inclusion and economic develop-ment, particularly the Organisation for Economic Cooperation and Development (OECD). The OECD has been highly influential in sponsoring lifelong learning, as a key conduit to the knowledge society and the information economy. It holds that lifelong learning is a key element in fostering democratic participation and citizenship, as well as social and economic well-being (OECD, 1996). The definitions of lifelong learning are varied, but the OECD definition is useful: '[Lifelong learning includes] all purposeful learning, from the cradle to the grave, that aims to improve knowledge, and competencies, for all individuals who wish to participate in learning activities' (OECD, 2003: 1).

It has become a commonplace term with policy makers, training agencies and the corporate world, linked closely with the Lisbon Strategy on the Knowledge Age, which led to the *Memorandum on Lifelong Learning* (European Commission, 2000). The Lisbon Strategy, formulated in 2000, holds that economic growth, social inclusion and sustainable development are contingent on the knowledge society, and has devised an agenda for lifelong learning to promote learning. This strategy has underpinned the developments in individual EU countries and has been very influential in setting the agendas on national development plans. Further, it has connected civil society with the economy inextricably, a result that is positive in bringing the economy out into the public domain, where it can be scrutinized and regulated more closely. That is, the economy has been perceived as being governed by irrefutable internal laws, such as the law of supply and demand. In civil society these laws can be interrogated, especially in relation to initiatives such as fair trade or minimum wages. Thus, the Lisbon Strategy, by promoting learning as participation in civil society, has, intentionally and unintentionally, incorporated a built-in process of evaluation and review.

The Bologna Process, again underpinned by the lifelong learning agenda within the knowledge society, focuses on the universities, and their role in constructing the knowledge society. A key outcome of the Bologna Process is the Qualifications Framework, which aims to provide an internationally recognized framework of educational credentials. The effects of this framework are to ensure transparency across Europe. This is a key response to the elitism of the traditional qualifications for traditional students, which is very resistant to the needs of non-traditional learners.

This means that lifelong learning takes a foothold in the formal system. Alongside this, it has provided a recognizable umbrella for adult and community education, together with an implicit acknowledgement of the value and worth of the processes and methods that make adult and community education so effective. In addition, adult and community education has long promoted access and support for non-traditional learners in third level education, but it has taken the lifelong learning agenda to guarantee this. Thus, while the policy development in lifelong learning has been driven by the emergence of the knowledge economy, the policy proliferation has created a fertile ground on which adult and community education can grow and flourish.

However, it has not been fully embraced by the education world *per se*. It endeavours to bring the disparate dimensions of schooling, training and education into one broad, umbrella concept, and to develop a unified proposition of existing systems, while simultaneously aiming to extend and deepen the understanding of learning in human, community and social development. This has several implications. The era of lifelong learning as been a long time dawning (Tight, 2002: 41). The first attempts that were made to scope the field occurred in the early part of the twentieth century, which recognized that learning could continue throughout life, and not just in the early years. However, the 1990s saw a more concerted effort to integrate lifelong learning into the thinking about education and learning, arising from the emergence of the notion of the learning society and the knowledge economy (Field, 2001: 11). This effort has drawn on needs of the economy in modern societies to develop the skills of workers, and to introduce them to new technologies and work practices. For example, technological changes have been so rapid in the first decade of the twenty-first century, that training is obsolete within a few years. In addition, teamwork has come under the spotlight as a way of increasing efficiency and motivation. The workers acquire new knowledge for these developments through training and up-skilling. Moreover, the growth in the needs of communities and individuals for access to skills and expertise in new developments in civil society, also calls on lifelong learning. For example, many people are involved in voluntary community activity, such as management committees in schools, sports clubs, professional agencies and so on, and they need to be aware of the processes and legalities involved. Lifelong learning is the way to describe these progressions.

Along with the era of lifelong learning, we have the era of 'lifewide learning'. Lifewide learning tries to describe a type of portfolio of learning, learning for all aspects of our lives (Government of Ireland, 2000: 32). When we answer the question: 'what do you do?' we might fall into the trap of saying what we work at, for example, 'I teach', or 'I am a lollipop lady'. Indeed, it was once very common for women working at home to answer 'I don't do anything', sometimes adding, 'I'm a housewife', in reply to this question. However, we know that our lives are much more complex and multifaceted than a simple reduction to the way we put bread on the table. Most human activity, from parenting to gardening, from current affairs to affairs of the heart, is highly developed and evolved, located in intricate environments, both private and public. For example, parenting of the young would seem to be a perennial human activity, necessary across the entire history of humanity, in all cultures, across all divides. Yet, when we explore parenting over a very short time-scale of about one hundred years, it shows that all kinds of forces can underpin dramatic changes, while simultaneously attending to the need to care for and nurture children. Parenting in the early part of the twentieth century was very different to present day parenting. This is due to the development of child psychology; the development of thinking about authority; the emergence of human rights, particularly the rights of the child; the women's movement; and, more recently, the men's movement. Even if the words are the same, the meanings have changed. The love of parents for children meant sternness, strictness and discipline at one time, while it was indulging, cosseting and pandering to them at anther time. Indeed, parenting as a joint venture is quite new as an idea, and, traditionally, society attributed very different qualities to motherhood and father-hood. Thus, this essential human activity of taking care of the children is a complicated vocational occupation, steeped in the values of the time. This work is highly skilled and demanding and parents quite often have to learn how to do it. But parenting is simply one practice among many others in a normal life. People cook, they exercise, they decorate their homes, they enhance their communities, they join drama groups, they join book clubs, they watch TV, they update their ICT skills, they try new wines, they travel to other countries, as well as doing their daily grind. This is the context for lifewide learning. The skills and competences to fulfil our needs in modern society are quite distinct from the early learning of schooldays. Lifewide learning aims to develop a base for learning for all aspects of life, to balance it, opening the access to new thinking on all kinds of subjects.

In order to ensure that lifelong learning equips people to engage as critical citizens, it is vital to have a critical dimension (Field, 2005). The concept of 'lifedeep learning' describes the learning at the deeper level. Lifedeep learning aims to go beneath the surface, to open the access to critical analysis, and to get a deeper understanding of the knowledge that underpins lifelong and lifedeep learning (Government of Ireland, 2000: 32). In the lifedeep dimension, you will find philosophy, media studies, cultural studies, equality studies and so on. For example, in a lifewide dimension, you may sign up for a basic cookery course in your local adult education centre, to get new skills. But you will also have signed up for a leisure activity that gets you out of the house and into a new environment. You will meet new people. You may decide to sign up for an advanced course subsequently, but that is as far as it goes. If this was in the lifedeep dimension, you may learn about the ethics of food production or the fairness of the market or the carbon footprint of some of the ingredients. You could also learn about nutrients and diet, certainly, such that you could decipher misleading information on food labelling. In other words, lifedeep learning would expose you to the deeper aspect of the content of the course, and you would expect to think about the subject differently as a result. For some learners and facilitators, lifedeep learning also includes a spiritual element in their learning. This might include meditation, yoga and other such courses. Overall, lifedeep learning aims to enable learners to excavate beneath the surface, to take a step back, and to take a more distanced, thoughtful and even sceptical perspective.

Thus, there are three dimensions to this overall idea of lifelong learning, which depict the linear trajectory of early childhood education to late in life learning, the spectrum of lifewide learning for a balanced life, and the multi-layered, meaningful possibilities opened up by lifedeep learning. This richness of possibility and opportunity necessarily raises the question: who conveys these opportunities, and how is lifelong learning carried into the learning environment? The next section will look at the purveyors of lifelong learning as it applies to adult learning, especially adult learning in groups: the educators.

Adult and community educators

I am prejudiced, of course, but most of the adult educators I know, in the community of practice that we shape, are courageous, dedicated and committed, connecting with the participants in meaningful and profound ways. But who are these saints? When we hear the term 'teacher', our comprehension is based on the fairly universal experience of going to school. We know it involves a person doing a job in a classroom. The perception of the job of teaching is located in the times we live in. For example, one of the major preoccupations of schooling is that of discipline. In the days of corporal punishment, teachers were quite often defined by their use of punishment, whether they were brutes or they were kind. In these days, keeping control in the classroom is a most topical part of the job, and people define teachers as good or not depending on how they can keep unruly schoolchildren in check. Yet many teachers love their work and they feel a real affinity with the students, speaking about them with passion and pride. The work of teaching is rewarding and meaningful, and the real dividends for teachers are when students do well, rather than any personal advancement for themselves. Thus, the job of teaching is the practice of people dedicated to service to others, imparting knowledge to the students, while creating the optimum environment for this exchange.

On the other hand, there is a lot of uncertainty about the work of adult educators. Indeed, it is almost an invisible job. When we speak about adult and community education, we talk about its role in promoting participative democracy and building active citizenship. It provides a second chance to early school-leavers and fills the skills gap in the economy. In terms of participants, we speak about the achievements of individuals in overcoming disadvantage, in changing careers, or indeed, how groups or individuals benefit from adult education, for example families and communities. For their part, adult educators attribute success to the students and participants. And when we look at adult students, we consider their achievements in terms of self-direction, learning instead of teaching. That is, adult educators do not have that prominent place in the system or in participants' lives that teachers have in the lives of younger students. Nevertheless, without adult educators, the learning process would not occur and the content of the programmes would be entirely different. Adult and community educators are in a dialectical relationship with the participants and the knowledge base, mediating between them, enabling the learners to engage with the knowledge and empowering them to create meaningful connections with it. Most of the knowledge is already recorded in books, the media and so on. Learners could access it themselves. But adult educators are not substitutes for reading or viewing a TV programme. Their role is to be experts in their subjects, of course, but they also have to hold the overview of the entire process. They draw on social and cultural analyses in their practice, ensuring that learners have constant access to the Big Picture, the macro dimensions of society; even though learners' lived experience is at the personal and microscopic dimensions. Otherwise, adults learning in groups are merely acquiring or consuming knowledge, rather than growing and developing. Nevertheless, adult educators facilitate that growth and development, and are generally very happy when the learners take pride in their own achievements. They are mainly self-effacing, and are happy, by and large, to accept that the work is its own reward.

Adult educators include those who work in formal adult education, that is, in formal courses with assessments, assessors and qualifications attached to them. It also includes adult educators who work in the non-formal arena, in courses that do not necessarily lead to qualifications, such as personal development or active citizenship type programmes. Adult educators also include those involved in training, that is, teaching or otherwise imparting skills or technical knowledge to other adults. Increasingly, adult education methods are adopted and adapted in higher education, with traditional and non-traditional students, especially in tutorials or small group learning. However, when adult educators work in higher education, they do not turn into lecturers. Adult education problematizes lecturing as a teaching method, questioning why it is so persistent. Lecturing is still the central plank in teaching in higher education, in spite of the well-founded suspicion that most people cannot listen without breaking their concentration for more than about twenty minutes or so. Adult and community educators reduce inputs to twenty minutes or less, and encourage discussion to enable participants to engage with the inputs. My colleague, Anne B. Ryan and I (2000: 95), urge lecturers to refrain from talking all the teaching time, and to actively encourage students to analyse and comment on the knowledge content. The key characteristic of adult and community educators is that they actively create the fora for mutual investigation and interrogation of knowledge and the subsequent creation of new perspectives.

The next section will consider those with whom adult educators work, the adults in the adult learning groups.

Adults in adult learning groups

When I speak of adults, I mean all adults. Adult learners range from early school leavers to senior citizens. The oldest person I worked with was 82, and one of my colleagues worked with a woman who was 101. Usually, though, we mean everyone over the age of 16. Of course, there are many people under the age of 16 who are more adult than many adults, but this book assumes that adults have life experience to draw on, and have had time to think about these experiences. Young adults usually benefit from this assumption. Adult education group methodologies can be used to excellent effect in formal education, especially the final years of second level. As students reach the later stages of second level schooling, they are regarded as adults in many aspects of their lives, including the right to privacy and the freedom to drive, perhaps even the right to vote, yet schooling is still structured to meet the needs of 12-year-olds. When these young adults enter the work place, they immediately take their place alongside their co-workers, and they manage to live up to expectations, in the main. Similarly, if they go to third level education, they enter a system that expects them to be self-motivated, independent and self-reliant. Thus, in the final years of secondary schooling, students are young adults, in comparison to the early years. In many ways, second level teachers are already working out of this assumption and this handbook will provide an invaluable resource for them. It will also encourage those working in specific educational projects designed to target early school leavers, trained in traditional teaching methods.

Higher education is also a changed environment. Mature students are increasingly prominent in third level populations, and they necessarily challenge the traditional hierarchical relationships between students and lecturers. This book draws on thinking that also challenges traditional hierarchical relationships, and will help staff to understand these processes and to transform their perceptions, if necessary. It is also a changing environment for traditional students. Making tutorials, small classes, small groups and so on, dynamic and conversational is often seen as a mysterious process that magically happens on rare occasions. An adult education approach can change that entirely, and make the process more interesting for the staff as well as the students. This book will be very helpful to those who want to facilitate this change and implement adult education approaches in higher education.

I also include adults with intellectual disabilities in this context, especially those who have the capacity to reflect on their experience. I have worked with people with intellectual disabilities and have found that this adult education approach is generally appropriate for their needs. This also holds for all adult learning groups, with or without disabilities, and part of the process of working with learning groups is to reflect on our own practice. So, at all times, we observe our own work, aiming to improve it and enhance our working lives.

Adult learning in groups occurs in a huge range of environments.

Adult education is a very popular leisure activity for many people dedicated to improving their minds, learning new ideas, developing themselves and participating in the social processes involved in adult education. In many ways, it is the mirror image of the gym but for the brain, guaranteeing results for effort. Adult education is also very important for people who consider that they did not reach their full potential when they were in formal education embarking on programmes for qualifications or skills. In my experience, many people have changed their lives fundamentally through study as adults. In addition, effective and interesting adult education programmes have been established for people with social issues, such as addictions, in which participants have come to see their problems through a very different lens, enabling them to deal with them with a different perspective. In adult education there are sub-genres as well, such as women's community education, a movement of programme organizers and participants who have developed an approach to adult learning firmly dedicated to improving their lives substantially. This is congruent with adult literacy education, aimed at people who want to improve their literacy and numeracy skills, with the intention of improving the quality of their lives and raising awareness about the issue. This is also congruent with adult education specifically aimed at workers who missed out on education early on, such as the Workers Education Association, again with the mission of changing the status of the participants. Further, there is a large cohort of people who are studying to gain entry to university education, or workers building on their qualifications for personal and professional development.

Thus, when I speak of adults learning in groups, I am including people studying in an array of systems: schools, colleges and universities; in specifically dedicated adult learning centres; in community, training centres, the workplace or trade unions facilities; in institutions designed for people with disabilities; and in living rooms, libraries, museums, pubs and clubs. Indeed, anywhere that adults gather, it is possible to create a learning opportunity. And this book aims to assist those who facilitate those learning opportunities.

It is also for adult learners, to help them to look reflectively at their experience of learning in groups.

Adult learners

Peter Jarvis points out that teachers speak in terms of teaching mathematics or art, that is, their subjects, rather than people who are their students or pupils (2006: 32). However, adult and community education is entirely learner centred, not subject centred, and adult educators nearly always speak of themselves as working with adults, not teaching a subject. As such, learners are much more than acquirers of knowledge. They sign up for classes to enhance and improve themselves, to help them to develop, to become the people they were meant to be. They include people from a myriad of backgrounds, and their experience of adult and community education changes them. They include students and trainees. Ideally, adult and community education starts with where the learners are, facilitating them to relate it to wider society. It consequently becomes part of their identity, and it shapes their views of the world. Thus, when adult learners sit in the learning circle, they are on the cusp of change and development.

Adult learning

Theories of learning abound, mainly based on how children learn or how animals learn. In adult and community education, these theories do not always satisfactorily illuminate how adults learn. Adult and community education takes the perspective that adult learning is fundamentally social. That is, even if a person is self-taught, they are drawing on knowledge generated outside of themselves, engaging with their experience in the world, and reflecting on that experience in an indisputably human way. Jarvis undertakes the attempt to develop a comprehensive theory of human learning, based on his years of work with adults. He tends towards an existential view. In this, he tries to express the complex set of processes that occurs in human learning. These processes include those of the body and mind, and are based on experience, largely conscious experience. The interaction of these processes, knowledge, experience and reflection lies at the heart of being human. Further, we exist in the social world, and the social world creates and gives meaning to experience, through the norms and values of society (Jarvis, 2006: 3–8). This comprehensive premise goes well beyond the idea that learning is something that occurs in the brain of an individual person, with no reference to the influence of the social world: the family, community and the wider social institutions, particularly the media. It goes well beyond the idea of training, which entails that an individual person repeats a behaviour until it becomes habitual. And it goes beyond the idea that human learning only occurs in school or college.

This comprehensive perspective is capable of interpreting what happens in adult learning, which less complex perspectives cannot. In adult learning groups, experience is the foundation, the starting point for the programme. The facilitator provides some input, but as anyone can tell you, input is no guarantee of learning. I can listen to the inputs, but it must go beyond listening. I need to engage with them, to integrate them with my prior knowledge. That is, my process of learning in groups is a series of cyclical stages or episodes building on one another. It is the dynamic interaction between new information, generated externally, which could be a new experience or a new idea. This new data interacts with my memories, knowledge and reflections, accumulated in the social world of family, community, the media, schooling and so on. The integration could occur through reflection, thinking about it, on my own, but I cannot know the value or meaning of it until I make sense of it outside of my own mind, act upon it and test it. The final stage of this episode of learning is that I have changed in some way as a result. A very simple example might be listening to an item on the radio, which resonates with you in some way. It is only when you get more information that you can evaluate it. We all know that you cannot believe everything you hear or read, and it is vital to find out what is reliable and what is not. You need another reference point to check it out. This is the social aspect of learning.

This may seem obvious, but it is a controversial area. However, adult and community educators take this more comprehensive perspective of adult learning as the norm.

Reflective practice

To facilitate adult learners successfully, educators must constantly review their practice, learn from the learners through evaluation and feedback, and include their revisions into their practice. This means that adult and community educators question their work, asking themselves and the participants at the end of each session how it went and how they could improve it. They do this verbally or in written form, for example, using evaluation sheets or creative activities. Of course, reflective practitioners will have a longer perspective than the immediate learners will, and may decide not to include the most recent feedback into their practice because of a wider consideration. Nevertheless, it is still vital to include the activity, as the practice of evaluation facilitates the learners to reflect on their learning as well as assisting the educators. Finally, reflective practice helps to build educators' skills, knowledge and values. This is the quality assurance process for adults learning in groups.

Organization of the book

The book begins with this chapter, introducing the ideas that underpin my approach, drawn from my experience of working with adults in groups, and which I have reflected on, with the help of study and writing, as a critically reflective practitioner.

Chapter 2 explores the context for adult learning in groups. I will look at the theoretical underpinnings of groupwork as it developed within the disciplines of the social sciences, particularly psychology and sociology. Groupwork also emerged in social movements, particularly in the women's movement, and this has shaped the theoretical perspectives. The chapter will consider the work of key thinkers such as Freud, Marx, Dewey, Freire, Giroux and Bourdieu. It will look at groupwork in related fields particularly through the work of Carl Rogers, Wilfred Bion, and continue through the lens of feminist thought and community studies, thinking that emerged from consciousness-raising groups. This chapter is the most academic of the book, written in the more conventional academic style, providing the foundation for rest of the volume.

Chapter 3 explores the wider context of adult education. It will describe and discuss what I mean by adult and community education, especially in the context of the interest in lifelong learning. It will provide a brief history of adult learning, drawing out the links with social movements such as the women's movement, the disability movement and the civil rights movements. This chapter will help readers to understand the connections between the practice in the learning environment, whether this is in a classroom, community hall, the work place or any of the myriad places that adult learning takes place, as well as the more usual adult learning centres.

Chapter 4 examines critical adult education. This is the term given to adult education which aims to develop the capacity of adult learners to think in a holistic way, by engaging all the intelligences, including logical reasoning and cultural sensitivity. This chapter aims to examine in detail the part that adult learning has in developing the values in civil society. Class, race, gender, ability and disability are central issues in adult learning and teaching, and each learning group is composed with these factors as given. The process of working with adults in groups must be flexible enough to consider these factors, but not only consider them: the process must work with these factors intrinsically. The intrinsic nature of class, gender, race and so on, leads to the next chapter, Chapter 5, where I move on to the characteristics of the learning group. The focus here is on social relationships, in which I link the complex interaction of humans in groups with the outcomes of social movements bringing about liberation and emancipation, and deepening citizenship and democracy.

Groups are constantly changing and developing. Traditional theory conceptualized this as the stages of development, but thinking in more recent times has characterized these developmental stages as fragmented and multifaceted. Chapter 6 will explore these intricate levels and dimensions, endeavouring to draw theory from the experiential reflections on my practice.

Chapter 7 will explore qualities of facilitation. Facilitation emerged in the latter part of the twentieth century as a style of leadership and participation that went far beyond the old models of individualized authority and loyal followers. Facilitation enables groups to work towards a goal, maximizing autonomy and interdependence among the participants. Adult educators, in addition to their role as teachers and tutors, optimally facilitate the group members in their learning. This chapter will evaluate the development of facilitation, in particular reviewing Heron's work on styles, in the context of adult and community education. Adult education is about the process of enabling participants to learn, which means that adult educators have the responsibility to make the content of their courses interesting and engaging. Chapter 8 focuses on innovative curriculum design and evaluation. This chapter is very practical, with outlines, lesson plans and methods of evaluation and assessment. The book finishes with a compilation of resources, exercises and creative activities. These are very practical examples and suggestions for adult learning, linking with learning group development and different functions in learning groups, such as communication skills, or decision-making skills. Thus, the book reviews the new departures in adult education, taking into account the changes that took place in the latter part of the twentieth century, and looking forward to what we want from the twenty-first century. It appraises the theoretical foundations for groupwork and facilitation, and connects these with the other social movements which characterize the time. It demonstrates the practical aspects of adult education, and provides a resource for those working or learning in this field.

At the end of each chapter, I include reflective questions to help you to engage with the material. Questioning is crucial to critical thinking and journaling is a reflexive practice that helps to develop ideas. The technique is to allow a free flow of your reactions, which can then be organized into priorities and arguments for and against. See the activity on Hot Penning, in Chapter 9. The free flow shifts critical thinking out of adversarial arguments, which limit thinking into a dualistic over and back. The outstanding feature of free flowing critical thinking is that it allows for a much wider context.

A learning journal can be a notebook, pages on the laptop or a loose-leaf binder. The important thing is that it is a space to ponder, and that you keep it for later re-reading. Journaling is a form of invaluable experiential learning.

That's the book. I hope you enjoy working through it.

Reflection

In your learning journal, ponder the following questions:

- Think about the most significant learning you did. Was it in a formal, informal, non-formal or incidental context?
- Think about your experience in learning groups. What were your purposes in taking part?
- Was the experience different to your earlier experience of learning? Why?
- Can you identify elements such as class and gender that you experienced in your learning group(s)? How did it impact on you?

2 The wider context of groupwork

Key ideas: emergence of groupwork; groupwork in different contexts; difference between groupwork for liberation and mind-control group; community groups, consciousness-raising groups; perspectives and approaches to groupwork in adult and community education

Introduction

Just as each journey for each learner is different, the journey of groupwork is long, winding and complex. It all seems normal, even natural, for people to cluster together in families and communities for sanctuary and sustenance. To this end, it seems irresistible to gather in a group, to collect with one another and to work together. It seems part of the human condition to find comfort and strength in one another, to form teams and groups just to get through daily life.

Groupwork is an expansion of this tendency. Groupwork is the art of working with others in the group towards a goal, whether the goal is explicit or implicit. It is based on the notion that groups are imbued with dynamic relationships between members, which generate energy and processes that combine to create a synergy. This synergy is more effective than the total energy of the individuals in the group. As such, groupwork harnesses this synergy, and uses it for the benefit of the group and any project it is working on. Understandings about groupwork are more sophisticated these days, especially where sports teams and work teams are concerned, and where an outside specialist can pick people with complementary skills and abilities. Thus, when we speak about group-work, we refer to a number of qualities.

So what are we talking about? For the purpose of this book, I need to narrow the terms of reference. I am taking the following as the guideline for this work. There are three types of collections of people: an aggregate, a group and a team. An aggregate is a number of people may be in the same place at the same time, without any connection between them, for example, shoppers, or the people in a bus queue. A team is a highly organized number of people who are together for a purpose and who need all members to contribute to the goal. Finally, a group is a number of people who are together for a purpose and who know they are gathered together for this purpose and who interact collectively for that purpose. This book focuses on this final meaning, that is, people who interact collectively for a purpose, rather than a team, whereby people are selected to work together to maximize their collective talents. However, a learning group may start out as an aggregate, and the process of working together creates the group dynamics. On the other hand, a football club may select a team, and they learn to develop the process of working together in a highly organized manner. Similarly, work teams must get on with the job. However, it is possible for the teams to develop the characteristics that we attribute to groups.

The characteristics of a group include the following:

- The group contains people who feel connected with one another and who know they belong to their group.
- There are at least two members.
- A small group has two to ten or so members; a medium group has about ten to 20/25 members while a large group is more than 20/25 members.
- A group has a set of values or principles, which it sets down explicitly or implicitly, in order to carry out its goals.
- Over time, a group develops a culture or identity, which characterizes that particular group.
- Interpersonal relationships are crucial to groups and connections and bonds grow between members.
- A learning group comes together for an objective, goal or specific work that the members aim to achieve, such as a session, class, support, study, etc., and all the members are there for that purpose.
- For the group to be successful, it must balance the goal of the group and the process of working together among members of the group.

Thus, learning groups have lots in common with groups with other goals, like therapeutic groups, groups in social work, youth groups, sports groups and so on. The learning goal distinguishes them, creating a set of conditions that adult educators need to be aware of, in order to ensure a good learning experience for the learners and for themselves. In a learning group, it is vital to make the most of the experience, to get the most out of others and ourselves. This entails a high level of cooperation and collaboration, and the capacity to overcome difficulties. These are fundamental group skills, and the success of a learning group depends on the adult educator's expertise in embodying and exemplifying them. These group skills are the key to the group attaining its goal, in a way that enhances each member.

Groupwork theory looks at the phenomenon from the point of view of what happens in the individual person, and what happens simultaneously in the social contexts. Groupwork is now quite advanced and the language of groupwork is now no longer stilted and full of jargon. We are all familiar with words such as facilitation, leadership, conflict resolution, teamwork, group development and so on, and read about these strands in women's magazines, industrial relations material and sports pages. This marked change has occurred since the 1970s. People are recognizing that groups can be a source of growth and effectiveness, that individuals can develop their own endeavours along-side group endeavours. Most of all, this common knowledge illuminates the sense that groups are not to be feared in case they take over individual will and autonomy, reducing members to a type of lowest common denominator.

The study of groupwork is the study of how people influence, behave towards, perceive and relate to one another. It did not emerge as a distinct discipline until the twentieth century and more particularly in the 1930s and late 1940s. Groupwork grew out of a hope that social science would not just interpret the world, but could show how to improve it; how it could be used to create a better society, as Marx asked. It aims to bring together the personal and the social, to look at how individuals are in themselves, and how their attitudes, beliefs and values form, grow and develop in the social context in which lives are lived.

This chapter will look at the story of groupwork. It will look at what a group is, with some defining details, when we speak about adult learning groups. We will look at the thinking of educators who advocated working in groups before looking at the influences and developments and the eventual theorizing of groupwork in adult and community education.

An exploration of the terms

This section will look at the commonplace terms in groupwork that help to establish the foundations for this chapter. First, though, a brief overview of groups as social entities. Groups are prevalent in all aspects of modern society and very significant in human and social develop-ment. In 1887, Ferdinand Tonnies coined the terms of *Gemeinschaft* and *Gesellschaft*, broadly speaking, community and society. *Gemeinschaft* is the term used to describe a tighter, more cohesive social entity, than that of the wider, larger society, *Gesellschaft*. This is due to shared characteristics, like purpose, belief, and place (Tonnies, 1963). He looked at family and kinship as examples of this tighter unit, but as we developed perspectives on groupwork, it is telling to see clear parallels between groups and community. The key point is the part that the individual plays; while in the larger, wider society they are more likely to be at the mercy of huge social forces, institutions and the state, with little or no control over the processes. Further, as society is becoming democratized, and human, social and cultural rights are increasingly recognized, there is an urgent need to facilitate people to become empowered, and to ensure that power is more equally distributed. Thus, the smaller, more cohesive entity in community and groups is not just a descriptive concept; it is can also be harnessed as way of bringing about social transformation. And this is congruent with other sources for groupwork in adult and community education.

It is possible to trace the origins of groupwork to key philosophers, psychologists and educators and to understand the context in which they emerged. This context dates back to the European philosophers who were very influential in creating the intellectual space that led to the French and American Revolutions, to the development of the system of human rights, and to the growth of liberalism as a political ideology. The Age of Reason or Enlightenment, in the historical period of the eighteenth century, arrived at the time that Europe was emerging from the Dark Ages. The Dark Ages as we perceive it now, was one of witches, superstition, religion and irrationality. The Age of Reason established the foundation for civil liberties and human rights, the abolition of slavery and the beginning of political movements based on democracy moving towards a model of human progress based on logic, reason and tolerance. However, it is important to understand that these main thinkers were embedded in a traditional white, Western, patriarchal world. The social changes that took place in the latter part of the twentieth century, particularly the women's movement, challenged this institutionalized patriarchy and other forms of oppression, profoundly and irrevocably. This has had an effect on the ways we interpret the theories of the late nineteenth and twentieth century, and the body of knowledge that we draw from for adult and community education. Understandably, it also has impacted on the groupwork that prevails in adult and community education.

A group is primarily a social system, as outlined above. When we speak about a group in groupwork, we are talking about the formation of relationships between the group members. People know that they are in the group, and that other people are in some kind of affiliation with one another. The group is more enduring, such that it creates a set of values that underpin it. These values regulate the hows and whys of the behaviours of the group members, enabling them to become inter-dependent and mutually supportive. When we consider the group in this light, it reflects the socially occurring groups in family and community. The qualities of interdependence and mutual support attracted the attention of those who saw how groups could provide a wellspring of resources if applied to non-traditional social groupings. That is, these benefits could be replicated when groups formed for specific purposes, like working, healing, learning, playing and support. This led to the parallel development of work groups, groups in social work, and groups in psychotherapy and psychoanalysis.

Emergence of trends

The most acute problem for adult educators is to enable people to see the big picture. The big picture depicts the major social forces that shape our lives, while adult learning takes place in the small picture, the lifeworld. The ultimate aim of adult learning, indeed, I would argue all learning, is to help us to become strong and capable of becoming autonomous. Groupwork can create the conditions that enable people to engage with the big picture while continuing to interpret the meaning of experience in the small picture. This is the main point of groupwork in adult learning. It goes beyond teaching or lecturing, as one side of education, and it goes beyond individual acquisition of knowledge, as the other side of education. Groupwork creates the synergy between these two sides. Historically, many educationalists perceived the value of groups for progressive education, prior to the development of groupwork in other contexts (Reid, 1981). For example, John Dewey formulated a model of groupwork for progressive education in the early part of the twentieth century, which had characteristics including an educational purpose, a set of assumptions that underpin its work, and a developmental process (Dewey, 1925). Paulo Freire, probably the most important thinker in adult education, implicitly advocated small interactions, with the concept of dialogue (1972). In addition, Freire's work on adult education borrowed the concept of *praxis* from Karl Marx. Praxis is a way of working that impacts on the big picture. As we know, it is not possible to live in the big picture. Our lives are the everyday things that we do, our relationships, the ways we express our inner selves. The definition of Freire's praxis is the cycle of action and reflection, but this over-simplifies it. Reflection is a deeper level of critical reflection, based on a complex knowledge base, which ensures that the actions are ethical and considered. The outcomes of these actions, therefore, are personal, in that people act for their own real interests, and they are social, in that they struggle against the social forces that undermine the just society.

Another of the strengths of groupwork is that of social capital. Social capital refers to the benefits that emanate from the interrelationships between people. Bourdieu's thinking about social capital is deeply influential, in that he saw that relationships have social value, rather than a value purely for the private world (Bourdieu 1983: 249). Groupwork promotes interrelationships, and perceives them as having this capacity to build social capital, rather than merely creating a soft or nice working environment.

Finally, groupwork facilitates the engagement with knowledge, skills and competence that may be beyond the reach of people outside of the main educational streams in society. Giroux's contention that main-stream education is individualized, almost secretive, mitigates against social progression (1992). In his experience, when he tried to share his learning, his teachers accused him of cheating. This sent out the clear message that sharing, dialogue and discussion was inferior to the privatized process of the learner and the learned. Groupwork is an indisputable guard against this.

Thus, groupwork has a strong basis for its favourable role in adult learning, in enabling people to engage with the structures in society, and to develop themselves as agents in their own lives. Groupwork has the benefit of creating social capital, and it challenges individualized, privatized models of education. The early pioneers of groupwork recognized these strengths. In the USA, social work as a profession became interested in working with small groups as a way of reaching a greater number of people, but also as a way of reaching pre-existing groups, such as families, communities, young people and ethnic groups. By the mid-1930s groupwork was very important in social work in the USA, and people like Grace Coyle who pioneered groupwork courses for adult education in the 1920s (1947), and Gisela Konopka who believed that groupwork was a route to social justice (1962), forged the links between groupwork, community and democracy. In particular, they emphasized that groupwork is a philosophical approach rather than a series of techniques.

In Europe, Kurt Lewin (1948) was highly influential in contributing to the thinking on group dynamics. His insights into the interrelationships that infuse groups have underpinned groupwork theory to the present. He firmly located his theory in practice, the foundation for the key contribution to groupwork, that of the T-groups. T-groups, named after sensitivity training groups, enabled participants to supply direct feed-back in order to develop theory. In this, Lewin subverted the traditional divide between theory and practice, and furthered it by viewing the participants as valuable sources and co-creators of knowledge.

This is a crucial foundation for groupwork. In addition, it is also vital to recognize that groupwork is not simply a set of techniques. This book provides resources and templates for practice, but these are no substitute for reflection and self-evaluation. In order to help with reflection and self-evaluation, I will go on to look at the critical influences on the development of groupwork. However, before this I want to consider the difficult issue of when groups are used to control and limit people.

When I started working with adult learning groups, I was not aware of any of the theory about groups. Indeed, I was mistrustful of groups, having a sense that they were mysterious entities that deprived people of the capacity to think clearly and independently, forcing them to behave in uncharacteristic ways. Simultaneously, and inconsistently, I suspected that groups allowed people to indulge themselves, reinforcing their own high opinions of themselves. The activities of cult-like religious, political and social groups that got huge coverage in the media at the time reinforced these beliefs. For example, in 1974 an anarchist group, the Symbionese Liberation Army, which wanted to re-distribute money and food to the poor, kidnapped the newspaper heir, Patty Hearst. However, she stayed with the group and was filmed taking part in bank robberies. This seemed to me to be an example of the power of the group to take complete control over an unwilling person. Another very telling example was the case of The People's Temple. Jim Jones, a pastor, founded The People's Temple, a group aiming to bring about racial equality and social justice though religious endeavour. In 1978, the group moved to Guyana in South America when the USA authorities closed in on the group, because of tax and other concerns. Nearly one thousand members died through murder and suicide, as the authorities investigated further. To me, this was another example of group mind control. To make people, reasonable and committed to social justice, to take their own lives, or to murder those who refused to, seemed to me to be an example of huge power, and the power was within the group process. Obviously, I had no direct experience of these phenomena, but I still formed definite opinions about them, which took a lot of learning and reflection to unpick. For the purpose of illuminating these undercurrents, I will endeavour to identify those elements of groups that enhance development. I will continue with an overview of groups underpinned by a philosophy of liberation, linking this philosophy with some of the philosophy that shaped the twentieth century. I will briefly contextualize this in terms of social groupwork, teamwork in the corporate sector, grassroots groups, self-help groups and the related areas in education and learning, which form the cornerstones of integrated groupwork in adult and community education. I will trace their influence to the evolution of groupwork in related contexts, looking at the hope people had in groupwork for healing, for democracy and for a better world.

Cult-like groups

This section explores cultish groups in order to distinguish them from the type of groupwork that we are dealing with in this book. When I use the phrase 'cult-like', I am aware that I am using a term that does not have agreed definitions or understandings in the wider society. In particular, many people who belong to these groups would have difficulties with these meanings. The sense in which I am using this phase here applies to groups that induce the members, through different forms of persuasion and coercion, to change their values, attitudes and beliefs and to suspend their informed judgement. There were many examples in the 1960s and 1970s, especially in the USA, but also on university campuses, in business fora, in self-help groups, even on the streets, in Ireland and the UK. Cultish groups can be religious, therapeutic, commercial, patriotic or a combination. However, my purpose in mentioning cultish groups is to highlight that the kind of groupwork that I explore here is rooted in democracy and liberation discourses, not groupwork that controls and constrains the group members. The two examples that formed my impressions of groupwork, the Patty Hearst and the Jim Jones cases, show this dedication to social justice, at least superficially, but their control over people's minds and behaviour underscores how power can always be abused. The essential qualities that people need in order to avoid manipulation include the capacity to reflect critically, to have access to information and knowledge, and an understanding of the hidden processes at work: their own hidden agendas, and the hidden agendas of the leaders. Most of all, the philosophy that underpins the whole lot must be embedded in personal and social freedoms, backed up by rights and responsibilities. That is, regardless of the overt agendas the actual practice of groupwork has to expose the group members to the widest possible knowledge and information; it has to encourage critical questioning; and it has to facilitate people to manage their own development, in the context of personal and social liberation, but not at the expense of others' freedom. This is the aim of adult and community education in the context of social justice. We will now look at the two critical influences in the foundations of groupwork within this context: the psychodynamic approach and the person-centred approach.

Critical influences: the psychodynamic approach

This section will look at the story of the origins of groupwork as a distinct discipline, in the parallel tracks of social work, psychotherapy and social movements groups. The late nineteenth century and early twentieth century in the Western world saw an enormous upheaval in the patterns of thought that prevailed up until then. Prior to this, there was a profound belief that the world was safely in the hands of rational men, who would look after the people. Colonialism, imperialism and paternalism were the main conveyances of these ideas, through institutions forged with a higher social purpose in mind. These institutions included the governance and legal systems, which employed rational, logical argumentation. However, this rational world proved inadequate to deal with the whole well-being of the populations, and was not capable of connecting with human life entirely. Further, Charles Darwin's thinking about evolution, at a time of vast upheaval in science, in society, and in all aspects of political, social and cultural life, overturned the basic tenets of knowledge about the world, and his theories form the basis of our way of thinking about biology to the present day.

A key contribution that enabled us to think differently about humanity in the twentieth century came from Sigmund Freud (1856–1939). When Freud started his work on how human beings can be both logical and reasonable, and simultaneously illogical and prey to inexplicable compulsions, his work was considered appalling and shocking. Freud's key contribution, in this context, was the idea that human beings are deeply influenced by the family they are part of, and the relationship with their parents forms their way of interacting with the world. He maintained that human processes were not logical and were subject to enormous influences from unconscious or subconscious motivations for human actions. Thus, his spotlight on the illogical and inexplicable illuminated human processes that remain pivotal, if still controversial, today.

The implications for groups arising from this perspective are that groups have repressed hidden lives, which emerge, often destructively, when they are under pressure. Bion (1968) elaborated the role the unknown, the unconscious and the primitive parts play in this emergence, and defence mechanisms such as *denial, transference* and *projection/introjection* which are manifested in resistance.

Denial transpires when an issue, experience, or event is so painful that the person rejects its existence, or minimizes it, or locates it elsewhere. This word has become quite commonplace especially when dealing with very difficult issues such as addiction or relationship breakdown. In the wider society, we have witnessed a form of denial in the way the Western world responded to the genocide in Rwanda, or Central Europe. For many, it was too much to cope with, too horrifying.

Projection is commonplace in modern psychology, and it refers to the assumption that others have exactly the same feelings, opinions and values as you have yourself. The non-romantics among us see falling in love in terms of projection, the perfect connection, before reality kicks in. In Freudian terms, this goes further in the context of the defence mechanism, whereby the subject attributes their own negative, painful, undesirable and unwanted thoughts, feelings, motivations and drives to another person, group or thing. In the context of groupwork, the Freudian sense may be interpreted if you see two sub-groups or group members perceiving each other in negative terms. For example, with one group I worked with, two members were practically mortal enemies, for no real reason. As the tutor, though, I knew from their assignments, etc. that each was accusing the other of their own flaws. They both spoke very frequently in class, yet they each perceived the other as being dominating and poor listeners.

Introjection, on the other hand, is said to occur when a person or group identify themselves as having qualities which they perceive unconsciously in another. Again, taking the example above of the two participants, it was clear that they felt that they had helpful, healthy attributes, such as initiating a discussion, sharing experience, engaging with the topics of the class, and so on.

The final defence mechanism, in Bion's framework, is that of transference. This occurs when the person unconsciously redirects the feelings for one person to another, who, in some way, reminds them of the first. In adult and community education, this generally is said to occur when the participant has had a negative experience in earlier education and transfers that negativity to the new situation. Counter transference is said to occur when the misplaced defence mechanism is returned. For example, a student, Mary, may transfer the authoritarianism she experienced from her schoolteacher onto the adult educator, Anne, and Anne may counter transfer the passive role of the school child back onto Mary.

That is, this perspective takes the view that all of these defence mechanisms are working away in the hidden part of the group, and are manifested in disruptive ways – obstacles that the group has to overcome and resolve in order to reach their goal. For practitioners, it is useful to consider these elements. However, it is important not to attribute all resistance to a defence mechanism, as resistance is a very important tool in the struggle for equality and justice.

One very important aspect though, is that of the facilitator in adult and community education, who takes a very active role in enabling the group to work towards its goal, and will therefore help the group to overcome the defence mechanisms. Moreover, this is not the only perspective that prevails and I will look at another, that of the person-centred approach, founded by Carl Rogers.

Critical influences: the person-centred approach

Carl Rogers said

> I smile as I think of the various labels I have given to this
> [person-centred approach] theme during the course of my career
> – non directive counselling, client centred therapy, student
> centred teaching, group centred leadership. Because the fields of
> application have grown in number and variety, the label 'person
> centred approach' seems to be the most descriptive.
>
> (1980: 114–15).

This approach rests on a basic trust in human beings. Rogers considered
that there is a tendency in humanity towards a more complex and
complete development. He asserted that there are two related tendencies
in life: the first is the actualizing tendency in each person and the second
is the formative tendency in the universe as a whole. This echoes the
feminist slogan: the personal is political, with the added dimension of
progression and development.

Rogers considered that the attitudes and assumptions taken by
teachers, leaders, therapists and so on were effective in releasing
growthful and constructive changes in the personality and behaviour
of individuals. Complex and complete development in humans moves
from a single cell to knowing and sensing below the level of
consciousness to a conscious awareness of self and the external world,
leading to a 'transcendent awareness of the harmony and unity of the
cosmic system, including humankind' (p. 133).

This person-centred approach is based on humanistic principles,
particularly that of human rights. And the politics of the approach is that
it radically alters the power relationships between people. Heretofore,
the teacher, facilitator, leader or whatever, has power over the group, but
in humanistic frameworks, the principles of equality and independence
are primary, challenging any semblance of authoritarianism or hierarchical power relations.

Parallel to the challenge to external authority is the concept of
internal development.

Abraham Maslow devised a model of human development centred
around fulfilling basic human needs in order for them to reach their
potential, which he termed self-actualization. Humanity has a hierarchy of
needs, he held, maintaining that 'lower' needs have to be met before the
person can attain their full potential. He ranked human needs in levels:

- Basic level: physiological such as hunger and thirst, sleep, sex,
  relaxation and bodily integrity;

- Level 2: Safety needs for an orderly, understandable and consistent world;
- Level 3: The need to be loved and to belong;
- Level 4: Self-esteem and confidence, resting on the sense of achievement, competence, independence, freedom, respect and status;
- Level 5: Self-actualization, a state of self-fulfilment, in which the person has fulfilled their entire potential (Maslow, 1943).

The humanistic approach is very influential, and the language of person-centredness has entered the vocabulary of adult and community education as well as primary education, training and other developmental processes, especially concerning confidence, a central problem in groupwork, adult learning and maturity. Confidence is linked to the need for security, and contingent on belief in, and respect for oneself, and having a sense of being valuable and worthwhile.

A number of studies support some of the contentions of Rogers and Maslow. For example, Harry Harlow studied the need for closeness and comfort in an experiment on baby monkeys in the 1950s. He created surrogate mothers for Rhesus Macaque monkeys – one 'mother' was made of soft cloth, but provided no food, while the other had plenty of milk, but was made of hard, cold metal. The baby monkeys opted for contact with the cosy cloth monkey, rather than the food-providing one. This experiment would be too cruel for today's standards, but it did show that basic needs included love and closeness, and not just food. While the experiment focuses on baby monkeys, it illuminates the need for closeness and intimacy throughout life, and not just for babies.

Rogers and Maslow are located within a humanistic philosophy, which is influential in groupwork and adult education. Humanistic group method and process is based on the foundations of humanism and democracy. In this affirmation of values, humanistic group method may go against prevailing social values and even against prevailing practices in the helping professions (Glassman and Kates, 1990: 17).

The values and norms in humanistic groupwork have implications not just for the individual involved but also for society at large. There are two objectives in humanistic group processes:

- the actualization of each of the participants;
- the development of group democracy.

The principles that underpin humanistic groupwork include those that are congruent with human and civil rights. It holds that people have inherent worth and capacities, and that they are responsible to and for one another. They have the right to question and to challenge, particularly those in authority. Everyone has the right to belong, to be included and to be heard. Humanistic groupwork protects freedom of speech, expression, choice and autonomy.

Evaluation

One of the key critiques of the person-centred approach comes from those who have a stake in the maintenance of authority. Many feel that the majority of the population needs authority and does not need independence and autonomy. However, adult and community education upholds these principles of rights, equality and autonomy.

Maslow was heavily critiqued concerning the primacy given to individualistic tendencies, and the assumption that each level of need must be fulfilled in order. This is patently not the case for everyone, and many people with not enough to eat can both respect and be respected in their communities. However, Rogers was fundamentally optimistic about the more human-centred world.

My key critique is that humanistic principles are very welcome, but they are fundamentally individualistic. This means that these principles do not allow a class or gender analysis, and therefore cannot transform society. That is, humanistic principles overlook social, gendered and cultural causes of inequality. When individuals, acting independently, develop personally then systemic and structural issues remain unchallenged. If society is to be democratic, it needs to address social and gendered inequality.

Having reviewed two highly influential approaches to groupwork, I want to move on to groups in social movements specifically designed to address social and gendered inequality.

Community groups

Since the end of the Second World War, community development has been a key conduit for progress and development in marginal, traditional areas, particularly rural communities. Over time, the pragmatic initiative to improve the lives of those involved developed a distinct ideology. Community development is beyond left wing and right wing politics, forging a path along what has become known as 'The Third Way', identified by Anthony Giddens (1994). This was highly influential for New Labour in the UK. Community development aims to empower people to identify their needs, to develop social capital and to work collectively to meet those needs. The model of responsibility to and for one another is central to the concept, and it proposes a code of ethics based on this responsibility, the just society. It encompasses the rights-based codes of humanism, but goes beyond them, in attempting to build active citizenship, social obligation and self-reliance. In Ireland, we have seen community responses to many of the issues in society, which have emerged as the outcome of the state's inability to address or to cope with difficulties inherent in modern society. It is an alternative to the harshness of individualism and to centralized state control and it fosters self-expression and self-determination.

Community development, as the grassroots activity, has been a very powerful agent in raising issues around social and cultural inequality, such as poverty, discrimination, neglect and other disadvantages. Community development essentially entails members of a community – geographical or issue-based – working in groups, working together to meet the needs of their community.

Consciousness-raising groups

This is similar to the story of groups working together for social change. These groups are new social movements groups and, in contrast with the old social movements, new social movements are more likely to be gender, sexuality, age or race/ethnicity based, and are more likely to have to have their political sites in civil society, rather than state and mainstream politics. They are more likely to be ethically based, rather than interest based, and are by and large non-hierarchical, relying on networking and informal organization, instead. Further, they are less concerned with sectional interests and more interested in values, ideals and an envisioned fairer and just society (Tovey and Share, 2003: 449–51). Tovey and Share contextualize Habermas's contribution, in their analysis of the late modern Ireland, in terms of the youth, peace and ecology movements in the 'lifeworld' (Habermas, 1987) which are congruent with adult and community education. Lifeworld includes the everyday interpersonal relationships, within and outside of the family, where we are orientated towards mutual understanding and common ground. This concept is very useful in helping to explain the trends in new ways of living, in relationships and in developing the self. The emergence of new social movements can be seen as a response by the lifeworld to the threat control by the authorities, including the state and many other institutions.

Again, in relation to groupwork, these groups are more loosely organized in comparison to early adult learning groups or psychotherapy. Yet, these groups were very influential in the development of groupwork for adult and community education. They contributed to the possibility for liberation through collective work, in particular. This emerged in both women's groups and gay liberation groups, and so on. In addition, they consolidated the focus on norms and values within groups, establishing the practice of group contracts or agreements. These ensured that equality, respect, tolerance and fairness were part of the group process, while they worked towards their goal.

The key to liberation is consciousness raising. The group members, through discussion, inputs and reflection, see their world in a different light, making the familiar unfamiliar in this process. Freire (1972) advocated consciousness raising for adult education, parallel to that of the social movements. This is a vital intersection between social movements and adult and community education.

Social model

This model connects the personal with the political. It takes the foundation of the humanistic approach and combines it with the thinking that has emerged since the 1980s on community development and building (Connolly, 1999). The social model relies on the perception that members of society can develop control and power over their own lives, overcoming social constraints through consciousness raising and education. Adult and community education tends towards the model of the community of practice, in which each member of the learning group is reliant on others, and is responsible – at least to some degree – for the progress and development of the group. This position is on the continuum of personal, at one end, and social benefit on the other. Sometimes the personal takes over, while at others, the social predominates. But most importantly, the focus is on the problem of extreme individualism. Extreme individualism prevails when society and the state are disregarded, and the pursuit of individual goals is privileged. Above all, extreme individualism aims to avoid social obligations, such as morality and ethical behaviour towards others, and defends the right to ignore the common good. The social model moderates the individualistic tendencies in the humanist approaches, while giving a special place to relationships, understanding and compassion in the process.

Integrative approach

It is not necessary to adopt one approach to groupwork and reject the others (Schneider Corey and Corey, 2002). Many adult educators have an integrative approach, drawing on newly emerging thinking in human and social studies, and techniques that have developed in other fields. The essential thing for adult and community educators is to take into account that people in groups think, feel and behave, and that it is their responsibility to facilitate this.

Conclusion

This chapter looked at the wider contexts for groupwork in adult learning groups. It provided a brief review of the main approaches, the psychodynamic and the humanistic. It connected that review with the collectivity of community groups, and reviewed consciousness-raising groups. Finally, it advocated the integrated approach, using whatever suits the adults in the learning groups. In this, I have aimed to give a flavour of the complex influences which converge when groups come together to learn in groups.

Reflection

Think about your own experience of groups, not just learning groups, but also social groups, like a drama society or book club. Try to write about the following questions in your learning journal.

- Are there traces of any of the key ideas in groupwork, like transference, projection, civil rights, consciousness raising or liberation?
- Are there explicit issues around power and authority?
- How are you in the group?
- What do you get out of it?
- What would improve it for you?

---

3   Wider contexts of learning as adults

Key ideas: origins of adult education; essential elements; links with social movements

Introduction

Parker Palmer is one of those writers who inspire educators to believe that they are involved in a project that has a profound impact on people's lives and is genuinely intent on their well-being (1998). Sometimes we lose sight of this when we face difficult learning groups, expectations, programmes, funders. Sometimes, it gets so difficult that it is tempting to abandon it. Parker Palmer talks about how courageous educators are to face these difficulties. He knows that it takes courage to persist with learners, and to be alongside them as they achieve their hopes and dreams. Similarly, as adult educators, we know that this courage mirrors the courage that learners have on their learning journeys. This chapter looks at the wider contexts of these journeys of deep transformation, with an overview of adult education and perspectives on the fields.

In today's world, it is almost impossible to avoid TV and other media showing us how we can transform ourselves. Their standard of change, though, is different to mine. They advocate change with new clothes, make-up, plastic surgery, exercise and diet and so on. There are a number of underpinning assumptions common in all of these programmes. However, there are significant differences too. But the key standard is the outward appearance of the person in question. The outward appearance is linked to a norm that is established and understood, about what constitutes beauty, health and well-being. Some of these norms have scientific bases, such as the ill-health implications of excess weight or smoking. Some, however, have no measurable bases; they are simply reflections of fashion. This is especially true of makeovers for women, makeovers which focus almost exclusively on superficial adjustments, with the overall intention of making them appear younger and sexier. These superficial adjustments include make-up, hairstyles and clothes, of course, which change from year to year. The norms and standards in these programmes are completely in the present and are ephemeral and fleeting. For adult and community educators, though, it is fascinating to note the language and the ideas expressed in these programmes. It is very interesting to hear and see ideas that emerged in long, sustained and permanent work with adults popping up in the makeover programmes. Transformation is a key term, together with confidence, self-esteem and courage. The images used include the ugly duckling transforming into the swan, Cinderella, or mothers looking younger than their daughters do. Hosts, friends and relations cluster around the participants, congratulating them for taking the risk to transform so fundamentally and on their wonderful achievement.

This superficial standard of transformation is in complete contrast to that of the deep, meaningful, hard work of adult education, which does indeed transform people, but from the inside and with much longer effects. This chapter will provide an overview of adult learning, with a potted history of adult education and a brief analysis of the strands. It will look at the outcomes of adult and community education, and provide a thumbnail of a role it plays in human and community development. It will look at the role of reflexivity and dynamics in uncovering hidden beliefs and values in adult learning. However, the next section will look at this in more detail.

Overview and perspectives

The education of adults has a very short history in comparison to that of children. A very cursory examination of history shows that philosophers and other wise people emphasized the importance of teaching young people. The focus on education for adults emerged with trends for social transformation, from the French Revolution, through the labour movement, to the women's movement. In the latter part of the last century, adult education entered a new era with the recognition of the deficits of mainstream education but mainly with the emergence of the demands of the knowledge society. This chapter will explore these broad social trends, preparing the ground for the current practice. The aim of this chapter is to root the role of adult education in equipping adults with the tools of critical citizenship, to further their personal development alongside the development of society.

I will start with a brief overview of the origins of adult education and continue with the more recent developments, particularly in response to the European initiatives which, in turn, take the lead from older trends. This cyclical, dialectical story will, hopefully, inspire adult educators to progress the adult learning project, that is, to empower citizens and to enrich civil society.

The story

This is a brief summary of the history of adult education, which deserves a much closer reading, but which is beyond the scope of this book and my expertise. But it is important to know where adult education has come from, in order to plot the course ahead, as well as interpreting the current practice and policy. The story of adult education is closely linked with an optimistic view of people, a belief that human development is desirable and beneficial to society. Adult education started to gain a foothold in the nineteenth century, with two main tendencies, to develop citizenship and to strengthen workers' capacity to demand their rights. In Europe, Nikolai Frederik Severin Grundtvig (1783–1782), a Danish pastor, considered that the populations needed to learn the principles of liberty, equality and fraternity, derived from the French Revolution. He founded the model of adult education that developed into folk high schools, which become widespread in Denmark, Norway, Sweden, Finland, Germany and Hungary. Their main purpose was to develop citizenship, and they were innovative in that they were largely residential in order to serve the dispersed rural populations. They introduced people to modern entities, such as co-operatives and progressive farming methods, and they based the process on discussion and self-management (www.infed.org/thinkers/et-grund.htm, 2008). While their history is embedded in rural communities, folk high schools in Nordic countries today have widened their remit to include high schools for feminists, Christians, athletics, senior citizens, radicals and so on. Astonishingly, they are largely funded by the state, which perceives them as crucial in the identity and culture of the Nordic countries, and further, and perhaps even more astonishingly, they adhere strongly to non-formal adult education: no qualifications, no examinations, no grades, no pass or fails. Study circles – that is, a community of learners actively forming in order to enhance the learning experience and to support one another – abound in the Nordic region, and are deeply influential in cost-effective adult education. For example, in Ireland, the practice of study-buddies is encouraged for non-traditional students, and homework clubs provide a meaningful solution to some of the problems of traditional students in areas of disadvantage. Thus, the legacy of Grundtvig's vision is a fluid, flexible adult learning process, which promotes learning for its own sake and for the sake of liberty and emancipation.

While Grundtvig established the folk high schools for rural populations, another trend emerged in England, that of adult education for
factory and craft workers, that of the Quakers Adult Schools (www.infed.
org/lifelonglearning/adult_schools.htm, 2008). In Nottingham, the
Society of Friends established the first Adult School at the end of the
eighteenth century, for women working in the hosiery industry. The
main purpose was to teach the factory workers to read and write in order
that they could read the Bible. As the Adult Schools proliferated, they
reduced the emphasis on proselytizing and re-focused on education.
They widened the learning courses to include mathematics and
grammar. These Adult Schools gained momentum in the nineteenth
century but their decline rapidly set in just around the First World War,
especially with the emergence of the Workers Education Association, the
WEA. Their legacy, in common with the folk high schools, is adult
education methods that are still current, namely discussion and concern
with social issues. These were carried into the WEA.

The WEA was founded in 1903 to provide adult education for workers,
both men and women. The main objectives were to make up for early
school leaving and to continue with education for democracy, which are
still key to their outlook (www.wea.org.uk/aboutus/, 2008). The WEA
still provides a huge range of adult education classes for all adults and
they have shifted with the times, including the lifelong learning
language and agenda in their material. The WEA was very influential
in the early years of the twentieth century in raising the awareness of
workers of their employment rights and the power of collective action in
pursuit of those rights. The labour movement contributed to the
philosophy of the WEA, while simultaneously benefiting from informed
and empowered workers. Obviously, this led to the establishment of
agencies and other programme providers, but this needs a fuller history
than I can give here. I have attempted to contextualize the current
practice of adult learning and to demonstrate the commitment to social
justice. First, however, a short review of the origins of adult education in
the USA follows.

In the early part of the twentieth century in the USA, Eduard
Lindeman was laying the foundation for the future of adult education
when he spoke of education as life itself, rather than as a preparation for
some random future for which education was merely a prelude. He
advocated a much more fluid approach to learning, a profound shift
away from more mechanistic and technical models that prevailed, and
which still have a high degree of support today. He described his vision
as organic, co-operative and non-authoritarian. He championed getting
to the roots of preconceptions and discovering the meaning of
experience. Most importantly, in terms of the legacy, he endorsed adult

education in small groups and was concerned with *praxis*, the cycle of action and reflection (Lindeman, 1926) which takes centre place in Freirean models of adult education. However, before that, in relation to the USA, adult education developed along humanistic lines. This was led by another key figure, Malcolm Knowles, who articulated some of the characteristics of adult learning that we see nowadays. These include the notion of self-directed learning and the neologism, andragogy, created in the mid-nineteenth century and which he popularized. These are important terms and I want to explore them in a little more detail.

Self-directed learning is the practice of adults working towards their learning goals, with support, but not direction, from the facilitator. It is a model of the primacy of the learner, and probably downplays the expertise of the tutor. This is quite an important shift. Most providers and organizers of adult education, as well as learners, see adult educators as experts, experienced but not authoritarian, a resource to the group who provide vast amounts of skills, knowledge and experience to the learners. However, Knowles' thesis omits this knowledge and experience and simplifies the role to that of group facilitators, more or less.

He used his second idea, andragogy, in order to distinguish adult education methods from that of pedagogy, the method of teaching children. Pedagogy is the science of teaching, coming from the Greek for children, *pedo* (www.etymonline.com/2008).

This word gained a lot of currency and in some European universities, especially Lithuania and Latvia, it is the term used for adult education methodology. However, it has been less popular in the UK and Ireland. First, there is a big question about the difference between teaching children and teaching adults. For many people, traditional teaching methods for children were problematic, and the differences between children and adults obscured that power was the issue, not the age of the learners. That is, traditional teaching reinforces the powerlessness of the children, just as traditional parenting did. Andragogy was useful in drawing our attention to these differences, but the word is cumbersome, individualistic and not entirely transparent. I don't use the terms pedagogy or andragogy, generally in this book, as I consider them archaic. I prefer to use 'teaching methods' or 'adult education methods' instead.

However, Knowles was very important in developing the profile of adult education in the USA, which in turn led to the concept of perspective transformation, developed by Jack Mezirow, which he continued to develop (2000). Again, this needs a fuller history, but the notion of transformation gained considerable value as it prepared the ground for the left-of-field concept of consciousness raising. Thus, when Paulo Freire's work combined consciousness raising, praxis and social justice, he was walking a path that the foregoing cleared somewhat for him.

This connection between adult education and social movements was repeated with the women's movement, the disability movement and the community development movement, enhancing the beneficial outcomes all round. This will be explored more fully in the next chapter on critical education.

This section has summarized a vast history of human and social development, skimming over nuances and details that require a deeper analysis, but the purpose is to locate the current practice in an historical framework. I now turn to the current practice, contextualizing it with trends in society that influence the norms and values that prevail.

The current practice

The twentieth century witnessed huge changes in terms of the overturn of traditional power structures and the continued democratization of the populations. Social movements have influenced society fundamentally, particularly the women's movement. Education has taken centre stage in terms of redistribution of society's recourses. People's engagement with civil society is infused with the pressures of the postmodern world. The lifeworld has become globalized, connecting us with elements that were not even on our furthest horizons heretofore. This affects everything from our employment to our entertainment; our education to our private lives. When we reflect on the hierarchy of needs, our needs for feeling included, involved and engaged in our lives are prior to fulfilling our true potential. A number of key trends and issues surface as crucial for life as we live it now. These include the part that technology plays, especially in the ways we have to interact with it for the most basic of functions, like communication. They include social mores on how humans must treat one another, with bullying and harrying condemned as inappropriate and disrespectful. This is especially pertinent when we consider integrating new populations, with language and cultural facilitation, and when we consider very marginal people, young people deeply enmeshed in violence and destructive forces, directed externally and internally. The issues also include the need to live meaningful lives, to feel that our lives are worthwhile and valuable.

If the adult education world could articulate its main purpose in the twentieth century, it would have to be around redressing the injustice of the unfair and unequal society. The twenty-first century purpose would have to add to that the pursuit of happiness and meaning. This is a key concern for people, and it influences life choice and hopes for our children in ways that were probably never really possible in times of poverty and other constrictions.

The women's movement, in particular, has focused attention on the personal, the private lives of people, and the need to improve personal relationships. People no longer have to endure the problems of difficulties in relationships and can seek help externally, in the form of counselling and mediation, for example, and internally, through personal empowerment. This has brought a consciousness about what it means to feel in a certain way, how things seem to me, rather than what it might appear objectively to an outsider. Adult education has responded to this quest in a quiet, almost invisible manner. In adult education, I can learn about computers, digital cameras, parenting skills, interpersonal communication, assertive communication, counselling, psychology, self-care, coaching – indeed, it would almost be impossible to find such a complete response to the pressures and opportunities of the present day, except, tellingly, in a bookshop.

This section has described the scope of adult learning, in order to reflect the complexity and fluidity of the field, which may not be immediately obvious to those 'on the outside'. The next section will look more closely at the elements that create this scope.

The essential elements

In Ireland, The White Paper in Adult Education was published in 2000, heralding a new era for the field, but identifying a number of key elements of adult education that highlight the diverse purposes for the discipline. These elements demonstrate the role of adult education in society, as well as in the individual adult learner's own life. The White Paper includes the following elements:

- Consciousness raising
- Citizenship
- Cohesiveness
- Competition
- Cultural development
- Community building

(Irish Government, 2000: 28-9)

These elements are highly complex and reflect the spectrum of society, from the personal, through the community and the economy to the social aspiration of cohesiveness and cultural development. This is a particularly optimistic perspective on the human condition, containing within it the solution to some of the barriers for a healthy society, with adult learners intimately engaged in personal and community improvements. Optimism is a dynamic quality that may be difficult to measure or assess, yet it has a huge impact on outcomes. Adult education has a long history of work with marginal groups, such as people with disabilities, women, especially disadvantaged women, unemployed people, alienated young people and people with literacy difficulties. As you can see from the story of adult education, this has recognized the value of learning for its own sake, for personal development, including work skills, for social change and for citizenship. This is due to the dynamic relationship between the essential elements engaged in adult education, which I consider to be present in adult learning groups, overtly or covertly, and conveyed by the adult educator as part of their overall approach to adults and the facilitation of their learning:

- the personal, social and economic aspects of life;
- formal, informal and non-formal adult education;
- lifelong, lifewide and lifedeep learning;
- knowledge, values and skills;
- cognitive, emotional and creative intelligences;
- the mind, body and spirit/soul or transcendent aspects of human experience;
- experiential, reflective and active learning;
- intuitive, imaginative and logical functions;
- ethical, practical and relationship considerations;
- the goal of, relationships in, and environment of learning.

These elements are present in most adult learning contexts, regardless of the subject taught. They demonstrate a multifaceted field, one that is capable of addressing several aspects of the lifeworld simultaneously and capturing the multifarious purposes of adult education. This dynamic interrelationship draws together the scope of adult and community education. I want to consider now the contexts in which the learners encounter these elements, though the learning relationship with facilitators and their reflections on their values and attitudes.

Reflexivity and meaning

Positive psychology has emerged as a school of thought, and is quite congruent with the positive impacts of adult and community education. Positive psychology focuses on the healthy, functioning, wholesome aspects of psychological processes, in contrast to traditional psychology, which largely focuses on the unhealthy and dysfunctional. Adult learning has had a history of helping people to fulfil their potential, as outlined above with reference to Maslow, and it has developed methods of working with adults that enhance their well-being and promote their development and transformation. When working with adults, adult educators have a variety of methods available to use to help them to have meaningful engagements with their learning. On the positive psychology side, Martin Seligman has pioneered thinking on authentic happiness, a profound shift away from the traditional direction of psychology and an entire world away from the superficial happiness of makeovers. Seligman shows through research that it is possible to be happier, to feel more satisfied, to be more engaged with life, find more meaning, have higher hopes and probably even laugh and smile more, regardless of one's circumstances, provided that we have some control and autonomy. Further, Seligman showed how we become passive when we have no control over our lives. If we are unable to do anything about the loss of autonomy we learn to be helpless, becoming passive and hopeless. This has an effect on our mental health. It has a wider social application too. Entire groups of people can become passive and hopeless when social forces, such as unemployment, poverty, patriarchy or whatever, take control of their lives. They are not able to motivate themselves to change or to have the energy to make the effort. It is at this weak point that the superficial changes can prove to be seductive and entice people to seek hasty solutions to their deep-seated need for meaning. On the other hand, those who withstand oppressive experiences or structures through development, including adult learning, have more inner resources and most significantly have the belief that they are not failures or losers just because they are victims of circumstance (Seligman, 2004). One of the guards against enticement is reflexivity.

Reflexivity is the process of reflecting, but it goes deeper than thinking over an event or entity and trying to come up with an alternative perspective. Reflexivity looks at our own values and beliefs, and requires that we uncover our hidden ethical positions. The following questions assist the process of reflexivity:

- What is the value of learning?
- What is the aim of working with adults in a learning environment?
- What are your beliefs with regards to the subject that you are imparting?
- What are your beliefs with regards to the process of learning?
- What are your beliefs concerning the outcome of learning?
- What are your beliefs about the nature of society?

These are the questions of reflexive praxis. They alert adult educators and participants to the issues that need addressing in order that they have common understandings of the wider contexts of learning as adults. These hidden ethical positions can also turn up other hidden dimensions.

Hidden dynamics

Reflexivity permeates the process of adult and community education. However, it is no guard against the hidden dynamics, which may emerge in spite of the intentions of the facilitator. Brookfield (1990) understands the psychodynamic undercurrents in learning through discussion. He considers that dialogue and discussion can easily desert the rights-based principles and devolve into a series of monologues directed at the adult educator. Groups may start out with a democratic set-up, but personal and social inequalities intrude and may create a culture very early in the life of the group that is very difficult to transform. Group members can invest participation with considerable emotional significance and their self-esteem may be linked inextricably to their perception of their contribution. This aspect of groupwork may be the most significant element of raising awareness and transforming perspective in adult learning groups. It has been hugely important in women's community education and other successful social action models of adult education, and it connects the personal and social in a very tangible way. It is at this point that the obligation to take personal responsibility should enable group members to become aware of the unconscious forces at play in their interactions with other group members and to overcome them in the interests of democracy. Discussion enables participants to connect with the topic, at both cognitive and affective levels. It is important to create an environment where group members listen to one another, rather than valuing only the facilitators' inputs. However, it remains the facilitators' responsibility to ensure that discussions retain relevance and an appropriate level of intelligence. Nevertheless, the ultimate aim of adult learning is to enable participants to engage in dialogue, at every level.

Conclusion

This chapter drew together a number of disparate strands on the history of adult education, rooted in an optimistic view of people's development and their right to emancipation and liberty. It connected these with the need for fulfilment, in terms of personal actualization and the need for meaningful autonomy. It went on to consider the part that reflexivity plays in equipping people to counter hopelessness and oppression, both externally, for example from unemployment or poverty, or from within, regarding internalized assumptions about who is worthy and who may not be. The next chapter will look at these issues of oppression and worth, in the deeper analysis required by critical adult education.

Reflection

In your learning journal, think about the following questions in order to uncover some of your own hidden values:

- Are you surprised at the origins of adult education?
- What was the motivation for those who set up the first adult schools?
- Can you imagine the life of one of the learners from the early days, say a young woman in a lace factory, or a young man on an isolated rural farm?
- Try to create a learning journal for them.
- Think of how they differ from you.
- Pick some of the elements of adult education and reflect on what they mean to you.

4 Critical adult learning in groups

Key ideas: critical consciousness; dialogue; praxis; class; race and gender; critical pedagogy; engaged pedagogy; popular education; macro-micro integration

Introduction

Wendell Phillips (1811–1884) said, in the context of the abolition of slavery, that eternal vigilance is the price of liberty. That is as relevant today as ever it was. We live in a globalized environment, and we get news of death and dying from Africa as immediately as news of a next-door neighbour. We watch stories of human rights abuses on TV interspersed with stories of soap stars' lives. Indeed, we can have more information about the cost of celebrities' shoes than about the mundane, everyday grind of managing to feed a family on a fraction of the cost of designer water for a celebrity dog. This proliferation of information has a profound impact. It creates the sense that we inhabit different worlds, perhaps that 'their' world is unreal, in comparison to ours. If we do perceive that we are fellow human beings, we can harden ourselves against tragedy and suffering. This may be because we feel that we are powerless and unable to act. Further, we may feel that problems on the scale of famine and political corruption are so huge that an individual act could have no real impact. Critical models of adult and community education are committed to changing that sense of power-lessness, helping us to think about the injustice of hunger in the *world of plenty*, as the Live Aid song had it in 1985. That is, critical adult education is committed to working for social transformation through our own actions. The belief that oppression and inequality are anathema to human and social development underpins this perspective. Further, future greater good for humanity cannot be used as a justification for present tyranny and suppression of dissent.

This chapter will look at what we term critical education. Critical education is essentially a questioning and analytical model of education. Critical adult and community education means that the content and the process of the educational programmes enable people not just to learn new information, but also help them to see that information in a much wider context: who created the information and for what purpose. The process must also enable people to question the traditional relationship between teachers and students. Further, the process must also model the implications of this questioning. This chapter explores the conditions for liberty and freedom, and the part that eternal vigilance plays in critical education. It looks in particular at Paulo Freire's key themes of dialogue, praxis and consciousness raising and relates them to social movements. Finally, the chapter will lay the foundation for the next chapter, the characteristics of adult learning groups.

Freirean themes

Critical adult and community education centres on the work of Paulo Freire, especially *The Pedagogy of the Oppressed* (1972). He brought the elements of critical education together, a radical advance towards progressive education, as John Dewey espoused. Freire's ideas continued on a pathway he started himself, conveyed by learners at the grass roots, and theorized by Henri Giroux in mainstream education and the road less travelled; feminist critical education, paved by bell hooks, in the USA; and in popular education, which has a largely Latin American and European base. This chapter looks at Giroux and hooks and continues with a short review of popular education. However, before this we need to understand Freire's work – quite a difficult task.

Freire was born to middle-class parents in Brazil in the 1920s. This means that his family had access to resources including education, health and wealth, which ensured that they were independent. However, he witnessed poverty and deprivation around him, and that proved to be the experience of critical consciousness, influencing his work from then on. He became a teacher and subsequently started working with peasants who could not read or write, in order that they could vote, and thereby change the political conditions of the country. Within a short time, this work was considered a threat to the state and he was imprisoned, but he continued the work after his release in other countries of South America (http://freire.education.mcgill.ca/node/37, 2008).

Freire's main work parted company with traditional education on two fronts. First, his most radical work was adult education. That is, his model for critical education targeted adults, engaging them in the project of changing society, not merely extending their citizenship or enhancing their rights, which were the two key strands prior to his work.

This chapter explores this theme throughout, but before continuing with the extended analysis of how people gain the sense of empowerment through critical adult education, I want to focus on the second parting of the ways with traditional education. This was around the relationship between the teachers and students. Again, in the educational models up until Freire, the teacher was the authority and the student was the subordinate. He called this 'Banking Education', a metaphor for the talking teacher, and the listening student. 'The teacher talks about reality as if it were motionless, static, compartmentalized and predictable. His (*sic*) task is to "fill" the students with the contents of his narration' Freire, 1972: 45).

This subversion of the traditional difference between the knowing teacher and the ignorant student brought profound implications for teaching and learning. In Freirean adult education, the educator's role is that of a catalyst. As a catalyst, they help people to transform their experience from the familiar and unremarkable to the status of critical consciousness, which Freire's translators called conscientization, and what in this book I call, consciousness raising. That is, they help people to see their experience in a larger context, so that someone who has an individual experience of, for instance, feeling stupid, can see that as an example of a much bigger system of judgements about intelligence and ignorance, not simply their own failure. As catalysts, adult educators bring a body of knowledge to the learners, but that knowledge is only one dimension of the teaching/learning continuum. The two other dimensions are dialogue and praxis.

Dialogue is the most essential quality of relationships, as it is through dialogue that we communicate with one another. Indeed, it is so present and unremarkable that it is almost invisible. Yet Freire promoted dialogue to the same status as consciousness raising. Anyone who was around for the early women's groups will connect with this immediately. In women's groups and adult education, people tell their stories and enter into dialogue with others about these stories. Dialogue generates new ideas and new perspectives and co-creates new knowledge, adding to the body of knowledge that the adult educators bring and the learners bring. Knowledge is not static and motionless; it is dynamic and ever changing. Dialogue drives knowledge to new dimensions. However, dialogue is not enough on its own, which is where Freire's third contribution comes in, that of praxis.

Praxis has a longer history than I need to go into here, but I just want to echo my comments in Chapter 2, that the usual definition of praxis as the cycle of action and reflection oversimplifies the meanings of both. Praxis is the action and reflection that changes the world (www.infed.org/biblio/b-praxis.htm, 2008). The action in praxis is that kind of community activism that has social purpose. Meanwhile, the reflection is deeper levels of thinking and feeling on the fluid, constantly dynamic and complex knowledge base, ensuring that the subsequent activism is ethical and considered.

In the adult learning room, the adult educator and the learners enter a dialogue about their lived experience. I know many people maintain that this is no better than a coffee morning, degrading the value of both the coffee mornings and adult education. The adult educator relates this to the macro elements of society, that is, the big picture, drawing on their knowledge base. For example, many people lack confidence. They lack the confidence to speak as an equal to others, or they lack the confidence in their ability to do a task, or they lack the confidence to believe they are worthy of respect. In their dialogue with one another, they can share these feelings. The adult educator then takes this issue (lack of confidence) and looks at it in terms of critical questioning. What is confidence? Where does it come from? What does it do? Does it depend on other factors such as money, education, beauty? Do some social groups have confidence while others don't? Why? Questions such as these questions will entail extra knowledge, while others just need people to think about the big picture. Adult educators may need to go back to the books for some of the answers, or arrange a project for the learners to find out the answers. In any event, the personal experience of lacking confidence is no longer a personal failing. It becomes an opportunity to enhance people's confidence and to enhance the learning simultaneously. The learners can then act on this in many ways, from setting up classes in confidence building, to speaking with confidence at the next parent–teacher meeting.

Thus, the common phenomenon of lack of confidence, so familiar to some people that it is part of their way of being, becomes the learning point. It is the pivot for dialogue, critical consciousness and praxis, the central themes of Freire's critical adult education. I want to turn now to the two strands that developed from Freire's base in the thinking of Giroux and hooks.

Henri Giroux said that his working-class experience was not only discounted, but also disparaged in education (1993). In my experience of adult and community education, this is an experience shared by many people. In the USA, Giroux's voice has been very strong.

> The critical question here is whose future, story and interests does the school represent ... Critical pedagogy argues that school practices need to be informed by a public philosophy that addresses how to construct ideological and institutional conditions in which the lived experience of empowerment for

the vast majority of students becomes the defining feature of schooling.

(www.perfectfit.org/CT/giroux1.html 2008)

Giroux uses the term 'critical pedagogy' in the sense of the critical positioning and ways of working of the educators in the classroom, their praxis. He asserts that critical pedagogy attempts to create new knowledge by drawing from many sources, taking into account people's lived experience. It is fundamentally an ethical positioning, and it takes race, ethnicity, gender and class into account when analysing the lived experience of people (2005). This follows from Freire's critical consciousness, but Giroux spells it out with more clarity and he includes gender that Freire completely ignored. This also parallels the most basic process in the women's movement, that of consciousness raising, and the generation of new ways of knowing. Giroux recognizes that Freire was crucial in shaping the thinking on critical education and the underlying presence of politics in education. Most crucially, he revitalized the relationship between theory, practice and the struggle for social justice (Giroux, 2005). Further, neither Freire nor Giroux were simply proposing a method that teachers and educators learned during their training. They exhort educators to be broader intellectuals, not technicians. They place the onus on the educators to generate knowledge in at least three ways: first, in dialogue with learners; second, in reflection; and third, in their own studies. This is vital to counter the pressure on teachers, lecturers and so on, to stick to curricula and to get students examination-ready as the only criterion of success. Increasingly, educators embody pedagogies devised to carry out a curriculum, which is formulated in terms of what society needs. This generally refers to the economy, but the point here is that educators are devalued in their intellectual role and re-valued as examination preparation technicians.

Apple views this technical role as part of the overall decline of education as liberation, and the promotion of education as something that a person buys and schools turn into lucrative markets (1982). Further, the market/consumer dynamic pushes the individualistic trend to the logical end-point, that of the disconnection with the social and cultural context. It is most difficult to generate class/race/gender consciousness with the meritocratic system, and yet the meritocratic system seems to be the fairest way in which to distribute educational advantage. McLaren perceives that it is the role of critical education to forge this link, to work as an educator to bring the social and cultural into the individual learning experience (1989). Thus, the role of critical pedagogy is to develop educators as theorizing intellectuals and to develop critical consciousness in learners.

However, Freire also had a blind spot. His lack of awareness of gender was a major flaw (hooks, 1994). I want now to look at feminist education, by way of contextualizing critical adult and community education.

Like Henri Giroux, bell hooks was born into a working-class family, but in addition, her colour and gender were formative influences for her (www.allaboutbell.com/, 2008). She sees class, colour and gender as interconnected in the struggle for freedom and autonomy. Her focus on education as a site for this struggle locates her in the Freirean mode, expanding and advancing his work with feminist insights.

As I have already said, the concept of the 'lifeworld' is very useful in focusing on the main dimensions of adult and community education. Concerned as it is with the minutiae of everyday, (extra)ordinary living and the face-to-face realities of interpersonal relationships, it provides the wherewithal to study this sphere of human life. The feminist slogan, 'the personal is political' could be the mantra for this sphere and the effort to enhance people's capacity to act on their own behalf. The forms of self-understanding open to us are both private and public, part of the wider cultural discourses on identity and experiences. When bell hooks devised what she termed 'engaged pedagogy', she was weaving together feminist education, working-class education and race education to create the form of education in which people were engaged in analysing the minutiae of everyday life. In the lifeworld, the subjective world is immediate and significant. Subjectivity is the meaning we make of our life experiences. When you place subjectivity in opposition to objectivity, it undermines it, as subjectivity is perceived as less valid than objectivity. This seems scarcely credible, yet human experience continues to be seen as less than, say, scientific knowledge based on mathematical formulae. Subjectivity is at the centre of engaged pedagogy, and hooks sees the subjective experience of her life as a catalyst for education.

When she considers critical feminist education, hooks sees that this analysis of everyday lived life is her praxis, the practice of speaking about her own life to illustrate political points about women's lives. Further, these accounts of everyday life resist patriarchal and traditional practices in education, which remove education from the reality of people's lives. She contends that it is much easier to teach a complicated concept if illustrated with a story (hooks, 1994). Thus, hooks weaves personal stories into critical education, in order to start with experience, but to further it with feminist analysis, as well as class and race.

Women have long engaged with adult education, see for example, AONTAS (1991). Increasingly, we see the feminization of education, with more and more women participating and working in the field. Education suits many women, probably because it is organized on the human scale, rather than on some abstract notion of work ethic or profit making. But the process of trying to create spaces for women's liberatory dialogue quite often clashes with structures that mitigate against openness and women-friendly places. In many ways, critical feminist education does not fit easily within traditional structures. Feminist critical educators could demonstrate a new way of working, working alongside allies in the field of adult and community education. One of those allies is popular education.

Making connections

Giroux and hooks point to Freire as the starting point of critical pedagogy, and while popular education has a longer history, the current practice is deeply Freirean. Popular education, as its name implies, is education for the people as opposed to elite education. It is parallel to critical education. Popular education is concerned with how adult education can contribute to popular struggles for democracy, social justice and equality. A vital component is the commitment to dialogue between people as a way of making the kinds of knowledge that can usefully make a difference. Teachers and learners are equal partners in the learning process, committed to fully democratic relations, in pursuit of an actively democratic wider society.

Popular education is not simply populist education. It involves emancipatory learning rooted in the real interests and struggles of ordinary people. Popular education is overtly political education which is critical of the status quo and is committed to progressive social and political change. It has nothing to do with 'helping the disadvantaged' or 'the management of poverty', and everything to do with assisting in the struggle for a more democratic, just and egalitarian society (Crowther et al., 1999). In summary, critical and popular education are committed to praxis in the struggle for a better world, for everyone. It is a long process and relies on the adult educator to carry it forward as the conduit for the knowledge and the process. Essential to this task is the creation of critical learning spaces.

Critical learning spaces

It is an essential concern for adult educators that the learning environment be open and accessible. If participants are too embarrassed or ashamed to contribute, this means that larger social barriers are recreated in the classroom. The ultimate purpose of critical adult education has to be the creation of learning sites where questions and doubts are positive, active learning, not signs of failure, ignorance or weakness. A high level of trust has to be present if group members feel they can take the risk of exposing themselves through contributing.

The role of consciousness is extremely important for all aspects of groupwork in adult learning. It is central in Freire, with conscientization, women's liberation, with consciousness raising, and Marxism, with the concept of false consciousness. Adult learning, with the potential for transformation, relies on consciousness for the pivotal notions of perspective transformation, critical analysis and reflexivity. The 'Golden Rule' in adult and community education, if we can ever have such a thing as a single, essential principle, is that the entire process begins with the participants. It begins with their experience, their fears, their hopes and their perceptions. Nevertheless, if adult educators were to stay at this point, the whole endeavour would be fruitless. That is, the process of adult and community education is to engage with the experience of the participants and enable them to reflect on the significance and implications of the experience, making it meaningful for themselves, in the light of social and cultural structures. For example, many people who had negative experiences in school may see themselves as stupid and dim, saying 'I was no good at school'. In adult and community education, though, negative experience at school could be analysed in terms of class, gender or race as large constructs, or bullying by staff or fellow students in terms of interpersonal relationships, which in turn may have larger constructions. Thus, adult educators need to understand how these larger social structures impinge in the most intimate way with how people feel about themselves.

Macro-micro integration

It is not possible to live in the big picture. The lifeworld, the concept used to encapsulate lived lives in day-to-day interactions and inter-dependencies, in the hurt, joy, wonder and sadness of everyday life, is a world of minutia, the micro. Yet the large social phenomena of class, race and ethnicity as well as gender are categories that are firmly located in the big picture, the macro. Since the 1980s, sociologists have attempted to integrate micro and macro theories of society, the micro-macro linkage. Ritzer and Goodman look at the debate between various sociologists who plump for the macro or the micro perspective, but they assert that the founders of sociology were acutely concerned with the personal, private impact of sociological phenomena. Marx was interested in the coercive and alienating effect of capitalist society on individual workers, and Durkheim was acutely concerned with the effect of social facts on individuals leading to suicide (Ritzer and Goodman, 2003: 483–5). In many ways, the macro is linked to objective social facts, while the micro is more closely allied to the subjective. Interestingly, Ritzer and Goodman do not refer to feminist sociologists in this discussion. Indeed, in a short section to indicate the difference between personal troubles – micro – which affect an individual and those around them, and public issues – macro – which are widespread issues analysed in terms of social trends, they use the example of domestic violence. They consider that

> a husband who batters his spouse is creating problems for his wife, for other members of the family, and perhaps for himself (especially if the law is involved). However, the actions of a single husband who batters his wife are not going to create a public issue – those actions will not result in a public outcry to abandon marriage as a social institution.
>
> (Ritzer and Goodman, 2003: 487)

This is a very interesting example, as feminist analyses do not see domestic violence as a personal problem only. Feminist scholars claim that domestic violence is an aggressive manifestation of patriarchy, and any particular instance of domestic violence an expression of the patriarchy enacted by the individual husband. Of course, it does break the law, so the law is involved, whether or not the police are called. Ritzer and Goodman do concede that domestic violence could become a public issue if it had widespread impact on social institutions. However, they blithely overlook the evidence of domestic violence and the impact of this social structure on the lived lives of individual women and women as a group.

However, Ritzer does provide a useful matrix that can help to analyse the macro-micro linkage, together with objectivity and subjectivity. In an earlier work, he proposed a four-level analysis of society: macro-objective, for example, society and social institution, such as the law and organized religion; macro-subjective, such as culture and values; micro-objective, for instance, patterns of behaviour and interaction; and micro-subjective, such as individual beliefs and perceptions (Ritzer, 1981). However, while he labels these as levels, in fact they are co-existing dimensions in that any one is not prior to the others. This also circumvents the problems inherent in dualisms, where one of a pair is considered subordinate to the other, an acute problem in any discussion on concepts like micro and macro, structure and agency, and, of course, objectivity and subjectivity. Thus, his four-dimension matrix enables us to view these as equally co-existing and influential. Further, it lays the foundation for thinking about the purpose of this research, which aims to link the small-scale interaction of pedagogy with large-scale outcomes of social and personal change. But first, I want to look at subjectivity and objectivity, which is a central concern in research, and particularly, in feminist methodologies.

Subjectivity

Feminist sociologists have scrutinized subjectivity in a way that other theorists have not. It has grown out of the study of women's lives, taking into account the minutiae of everyday life as well as the overall trends that constrain women's lives. Women, and other subordinate people, learn to perceive themselves as inferior to the super-ordinate group, in the process of internalizing society's norms and values, along with the way in which the self as a social actor must operate out of established knowledge. That is, they are different to the dominant cultural norms. Dominant groups and individuals develop their sense of identity through feedback from their peers. Women and other subordinate groups see themselves through the eyes of these dominant norms, and therefore see themselves as less than them, inadequate fundamentally. Most of all, this disjointed sense of identity denies the validity of their own experience (Madoo Lengermann and Niebrugge-Brantley, 2003: 474–5). But equally, women depend on these super-ordinate norms for their formation. Further, subjectivity encompasses both the conscious and unconscious, and the myriad levels and dimensions that these have in people's lives.

> Subjectivity is used to refer to the conscious and unconscious thoughts and emotions of the individual, her sense of herself and her ways of understanding her relation to the world ... poststructuralism proposes a subjectivity which is precarious, contradictory and in process, constantly being constituted in discourse each time we think or speak.
>
> (Weedon, 1997: 32)

Thus, feminist analyses of subjectivity represent a highly complex set of elements, from the outside social norms and values to the internalized imperatives, both conscious and unconscious. We have an understanding of subjectivity as a powerful aspect of the human condition, rather than an inadequate, deficient opposite of objectivity. Further, subjectivity is holistic and multifaceted, including the rational and logical with the emotional and intuitive. Moreover, critical adult educators must critically question objectivity in order to shift it from the prime position as unqualified truth or uncontested knowledge and feminist research promotes subjectivity to locate it alongside objectivity as valid knowledge. But there is another aspect of the big picture that needs to be explored: that of structure and the way agency operates within it as well as creating it. For adult learners, this is vital. Personal change through adult and community education remains shallow and trivial unless accompanied by the sense of self as actor, agentic within their own life, able to make choices and decisions about their destiny.

Agency and structure continuum

Ritzer and Goodman (2003) locate the micro to the macro ends of social phenomena on a continuum rather than regarding them as opposites. They associate the agency/structure dilemma with micro to macro continuum, with distinct differences. 'While agency generally refers to micro-level, individual human actors, it can also refer to (macro) collectivities that act' (p. 508). That is, this characterization takes into account that agency can include collective action, and not just individual action. Their view of structure, similarly, locates it also within the macro and micro: 'while structure usually refers to large-scale social structure, it also can refer to micro structures such as those involved in human interaction' (p. 509).

Bourdieu focused on practice as the outcome of the dialectical relationship between structure and agency (1977: 3). If we consider the learning group as a site of practice, we can perceive this relationship in a tangible way. Reflexivity is an indispensable component of consciousness raising, located within praxis.

Consciousness raising and the big picture

Bourdieu is notable for the concept he developed of 'habitus', the mental or cognitive structures through which people deal with the social world, that is, 'internalised, embodied social structures' (1984: 468). With consciousness of both macro and micro aspects of society, agency and structure and subjectivity and objectivity, we can overcome the implicit determinism of powerful social institutions, but simultaneously we can recognize the extent of individual power. That is, we can overcome somewhat the power that economic, social and cultural forces exercise, such as economic booms and busts, which seem to follow economic laws only. We can prevail over economic laws by exercising personal and collective power, such as supporting fair trade or ecological practices that counter, at least to some extent, economic forces like the law of supply and demand. In order to develop this personal and social power, we need to develop consciousness, raised awareness of the 'why?' of these macro forces, in order to chart our course. I contend that adult and community education is an essential component in developing raised consciousness. Further, it is vital to continue to develop ways of facilitating learners to reflect as they speak, enabling them to be agentic in their own worlds, and to act upon the structural dimensions.

Conclusion

Critical adult and community education can disappear in the pressure to provide classes, to get through a curriculum and facilitate the learners completing their course. However, if adult education is to remain meaningful for the participants and their communities it has to convey critical ideas and ways of working all through that 'busyness'. The learners will carry some of these ideas, but it hinges on educators' commitment to justice. This chapter reflects on the place of critical ideas in the lifeworld of adult learning, and provides a rationale for educators to embody them in their praxis. It reviewed Freire's work and the application to current praxis. It provided a way of thinking about how praxis integrates the agentic and the structural.

Reflection

This chapter is quite difficult in terms of ideas that may not be immediately important to educators as they go about their busy lives. However, it is vital to think about what happens if you don't have critical ideas when you facilitate learners. In your learning journal, try to identify what is most difficult for you and why that is. Then, look at how you could integrate that in your practice. Challenge yourself to act as devil's advocate to your own beliefs.

---

5 Characteristics of adult learning groups

Key ideas: common grounds; diverse perspectives; psychodynamic approach; behaviourist perspective; humanistic approach; purpose and process; purpose of the learning group; process in the learning group; hidden purposes and processes

Introduction

When I started in adult and community education, in the mid-1980s, I had no prior experience of working with groups. I had been in small social groups and work teams, but I never really thought about what was really happening. I had a rudimentary understanding of what makes people tick, and that the process of working together could change how people were. I knew that something might happen that could bring about a change of mood, either lift the mood or depress it. The process could help to generate ideas or energy seemingly out of nowhere. I had attended a 'night class', which was an applied arts class for adults, located in my local post-primary school. This really was the beginning of my reflection on learning groups, as I became very conscious of what was happening and some insight into how it progressed.

For the night class, a group of about fifteen people enrolled with the local adult education organizer. These night classes took place in a local school, along with all kinds of courses, such as Car Maintenance, Hostess Cookery, DIY for Beginners, Arts and Crafts. Members of our group began to acknowledge one another as we tentatively sidled into the resonant classroom, with its graffiti love poems on the traditional desks, and the smell of pencil parings and paper. I strongly remember that we drifted towards the back of the room, hoping to fade into the background. I was wondering if I was mad to put myself back into the classroom, which I experienced as a form of excruciating torture the first time around. I was really unsure of the value of it all, as it seemed to be so reminiscent of my schooldays, and all for what? The familiar posters on the wall were not promising. While we waited for the tutor, we whispered our fears to one another. The uncertainty was palpable, a combination of the collective memory of the classroom, together with the unknown of the new course.

The tutor entered with a flurry of stuff: materials, laughter, chatter and ease. It transpired that the content of the class would consist of all kinds of needlework, and we could choose from a bill of fare what we would like to do, ultimately. The members of the class were exclusively women, eager to get out of the house, and the subject was vaguely familiar from our secondary schooldays in Home Economics. When the class finished at the end of about eight weeks, we looked back on the experience as a lot of fun, a lot of chat, many connections with one another, and we all had some passable, even beautiful pieces of work to show for it.

Arts and crafts classes are usually treated with the utmost derision, and considered the lowest form of life on the adult education menus, even lower than flower arranging. However, I learned a lot from this group, learning that has stayed with me since and has influenced my work profoundly, including being a foundation for this book. This chapter will look at the key learning from that experience and connect it with the discussions on the characteristics of the learning group and endeavours to link the macro world of that context with the micro world of the learning group.

The difference

When I reflect on the key differences between this class and the earlier experience of schooling, it helps me to understand the characteristics of adult learning groups. For many people, their reflection on the ways groups operate is founded on their experience of their early family lives. Groupwork in psychotherapy is located in this domain, based on a person's childhood relationships with their parents and siblings, and it is the quintessential starting point for therapeutic work. However, learning groups have distinct purposes and goals, which distinguishes them from therapeutic groups. The mix of knowledge, process and outcome in the educational environment is very important for understanding the ways learning groups work. In addition, the evolution of groupwork in other contexts had significantly influenced adult and community education. These include groups in social movements such as the women's movement and the disability movement; the corporate world, where teamwork is increasingly promoted; community development; and youth work. Thus, groupwork, *per se*, has developed since the mid-1970s or so, in distinct but connected fields, all of which provide inspiration for one another. While there are major overlapping principles, the specific adult and community education context is quite distinctive. But before I look at this in more detail, I want to reflect on the key difference between the adult education classroom and the traditional one.

First, there was little of the atmosphere of the remembered classroom. Here, we had no suppressed giggles; no undercurrent of 'them' and 'us'; no dread of the beady eye of attention; no undone homework for which we would have to make outrageous excuses. Each of us remembered that when we were in school, we were strongly discouraged from speaking to each other while making handicrafts, or cooking, or whatever, except for the barely necessary communication for cooperation. In addition, a loud laugh incurred a severe reprimand from the teacher, who considered it a major transgression.

In our adult education applied arts class, we sat at the old familiar desks, but that was the end of the familiarity. Instead, the desks became pivots for conversations, jokes and lots of fun. Very quickly, we were able to create a very convivial atmosphere. The teacher showed us many examples of what we would work on, and we started straight away, ripping out the mistakes, and praising each other for the successes. As we worked with our hands, the teacher used that time to talk about the history of the crafts, the origin of the yarns, materials and so on. When she was not talking, she strolled around the participants, commenting and providing help and support. During this time, we chatted about our lives, about our earlier experiences of handicrafts, drifting over many topics and areas. Thus, at the end of any session, we had learned a bit of history, some life stories of the participants, some environmental science, in addition to creating our own piece of art.

The instructor was very relaxed. She was gently directive when she needed to focus on the task in hand, and very fluid when we were all working and chatting. There was no deference to her just because she was a teacher, or nudging and winking by the participants, inferring that the teacher was super-ordinate to the participants, monitoring our behaviour. I learned so much from her. At the end of the classes, I had a beautiful Celtic knot embroidered on a piece of traditional Irish cloth, báinín, but I also learned how different adult learning was to school learning. The rest of the chapter will look in more detail at the difference between adult learning in groups and the traditional classroom, drawing together the strands of the previous chapters.

Characteristics of learning groups

In this section, I will discuss the assumptions that underpin learning and teaching in traditional modes of education, in order to highlight the disparity between those traditional modes and the more typical adult learning groups.

Society has moved away from the notion of the *tabula rasa,* the belief that children enter the classroom with their minds similar to a completely blank slate. Then, it was up to the teacher to fill in that blank slate with the knowledge and skills that would eventually equip them to take their place in the world. In the unself-conscious era of patriarchal authoritarianism, especially at the end of the nineteenth century, educationalists considered that class and gender were static and unchangeable, and educational provision reflected this. The 'Three Rs' equipped working-class boys with basic skills for work, while girls, in addition to the Three Rs, learned needlework and cookery to equip them for their domestic lives. The hidden curriculum also contained the two other Rs, that of right and wrong, the moral code based on the norms of society. The idea that they could all learn cookery, or that they would learn more than the reading, writing and mathematics did not come until much later. Indeed, in Ireland, remaining in school after the age of 14 did not become commonplace until the 1960s for working-class children.

Simultaneous with the belief that class, race and gender inequality was unchanging and normal was the idea of liberal education, aimed at developing the moral superiority for upper and middle classes, to equip them for their roles in society as leaders and elites. The principles of liberty, equality and fraternity were slow to permeate the norms in society, and the education system reflected that. Someone said that it is still too early to tell if the French Revolution was successful or not, that 200 years is not enough time to see the real effects. It is probably too early to see the impact on the education system, in general. However, adult and community education, as discussed in Chapter 3, on the wider contexts of adult learning, has firm roots in liberation agendas. This has a profound impact, manifest in the characteristics of adult learning groups. The next section will look at the characteristics that learning groups have with other groups, and continue then to look at the characteristics that are unique to learning groups.

Common grounds

In my experience, learning groups have been widely different from one another, and yet they also have a lot in common. This common ground has many distinctive characteristics, which distinguish the learning group from other types of groups. Learning groups have many characteristics in common with other groups, also, and this chapter will provide the opportunity to reflect on the similarities and differences.

When the spotlight was turned on groups in the early part of the twentieth century, it was noted that groups of people behaved in a collective way, quite distinctive from the way disparate individuals might behave, and people were different in different groups. That is, a group is a system, with each part interdependent on the other. Kurt Lewin probably coined the phrase that we are all familiar with now: 'group dynamics'. As the term implies, group dynamics are energetic, a combination of cognitive, emotional and physical energy. Lewin held that interdependence within the group, gathered for a common goal, triggered effects that affected all members and sub-groups. Groups are dynamic in that there is always interaction at some level, and group members influence one another, even if members avoid that influence. This interaction is a series of actions and reactions, and the dialectical progress of the group is a type of synthesis of each stage of action and reaction. This means that every member of the group has changed in some way, because of the influence of other members. This is the case even if we have no idea that it is making an impact. Alongside the impact of the other people on each group member, the group itself develops. Just as each person develops in their own life journey, reaching developmental milestones and then moving on, a group evolves and matures as it progresses through its life journey. Group dynamics cover these notions: the interactions and interdependence of the group members as the group forms into a cohesive entity, a system, and the development of the group over its lifetime. First, though, there follows a brief review of the underlying perspectives in groupwork.

Diverse perspectives

As we saw, groups are prevalent in all aspects of modern society and very significant in human and social development. However, it is possible to trace the origins of groupwork to key philosophers, psychologists and educators in the twentieth century. It is essential to understand that the main thinkers are embedded in a traditional white, Western, patriarchal world – even the founding members of humanistic approaches, which aimed for universal rights and freedoms, influenced by the radical philosophy of twentieth-century existentialism. However, an understanding of these diverse perspectives helps to illuminate hugely complex phenomena, and hopefully will equip you to think critically about groupwork.

Three perspectives dominate the thinking about groups and the way they work and these are influential in all aspects of groupwork, including groupwork in adult and community education. These are the psychodynamic, the behaviourist and the humanistic perspectives. This section will briefly outline each, and evaluate the elements that are beneficial when thinking about adult and community education.

Psychodynamic approach

I discuss this in more detail in Chapter 2, but here I want to look at the significance of the psychodynamic approach for adult learning groups. As I said previously, Sigmund Freud's contribution to the twentieth century was to help us to understand that everything in human society did not always unfold in a liner, rational, logical manner, a view that dominated Western thought at the time, particularly as applied to men. Females were illogical and irrational in this frame of mind, but Freud did not propose a female model of irrationality, but rather that people act out of hidden parts of their psyche. When we apply this to learning groups, two phenomena result: that individuals act in ways that cannot always be explained, and that the entire group develops a personality or culture, again, one that cannot always be explained logically. The implications for groups arising from this perspective are that groups and group members have repressed hidden lives, which emerge, often destructively, when the groups are under pressure. The role of the unknown, the unconscious and the primitive play parts in this emergence, and defence mechanisms such as denial, transference and projection/introjection (Encyclopaedia of Psychology, 2008) transpire.

Within learning groups, denial may emerge when the curriculum is very challenging. For example, group members may not accept social or gender analysis, attributing new ideas to a misguided women's movement or misplaced compassion. When we look again at the example of the applied arts class, if the tutor analysed handicrafts in terms of exploitation of women's work, many of the class members would have found that challenging, and perhaps would have dismissed the tutor as a crank or oddity. Yet we do know that fine craft work like embroidery and lace making is almost entirely done by women, and it is generally underpaid and undervalued.

Projection is commonplace in modern psychology, and it refers to the assumption that others have exactly the same feelings, opinions and values as you have yourself. For example, in 1954, Muzafer and Carloyn Sherif conducted an interesting experiment called the Robbers Cave Experiment (http://psychclassics.yorku.ca/Sherif/index.htm, 2008). This focused on conflict resolution, but it is insightful in terms of projection. The researchers formed two groups, completely randomly, and, after an interval, each group viewed the other with suspicion, for no real reason. This same phenomenon is quite common. I experienced it as a group participant, when we worked alongside another group. We felt that we were better: more intelligent, more fun, more engaging, more everything. As an adult and community educator, I frequently encountered two groups who accused one another of their own flaws. However, this could have other explanations. For example, it is socially useful to regard the unknown with suspicion or caution. This is a reflex in many ways, in order to ensure survival. Moreover, if a community is secure, with high self-esteem and a clear identity, it is much easier to embrace the unknown, without attributing any negative qualities to it.

Introjection, on the other hand, is said to occur when a person or group identify themselves as having qualities which they perceive unconsciously in another. Taking the example of my experience in one of two groups, introjection may be interpreted if a quality of the other group, such as that of being more united, let us say, was attributed to our group. However, it is difficult to identify an actual quality in such relative terms. It is possible that hostility or admiration is well-founded, rather than inexplicable drives or impulses.

The final defence mechanism, in psychodynamic terms, is that of transference. This occurs when the person unconsciously redirects their feelings for one person to another, who, in some way, reminds them of the first. In adult and community education, this generally is said to occur when the participant has had a negative experience in earlier education and transfers that negativity to the new situation. Counter-transference is said to occur when the misplaced defence mechanism is returned.

In terms of adults learning in groups, transference and counter-transference raise issues about expectations when people enter the adult learning group for the first time. Some of these expectations are explainable. For many people, their fears about their earlier experience are well substantiated. They *did* have terrible experiences in school. They needed to be very cautious of schoolteachers. However, if the expectations cannot be explained, transference and counter-transference may be a mechanism to interpret them, to help people to become self-aware and insightful observers of themselves.

These theories of defence mechanisms are very influential for people who have been trained in the psychodynamic model of groupwork. However, for people taking a more integrated approach to groupwork in adult and community education, it is vital to take a wider overview. Defence mechanisms of denial, project/introjection, transference and counter-transference are understandable using the theories of socialization, that is, the internalization of the norms and values of society.

Socialization is dealt with in greater detail in the section on purposes and processes, but I need to emphasize here that the defence mechanisms are seen as personal inadequacies, on the part of those who have them, while the theory of socialization sees them as the inevitable self-preservation of the workings of society. Furthermore, the feminist critique of Freudian thought and influence is compelling, particularly in the questioning of Western, white, male assumptions. Indeed, Freudian thought could be analysed in terms of his own thinking around unconscious defence mechanisms, especially with regards to the notion of penis envy. Could it be that men are unconsciously envious of the womb? Anyway, concerning groupwork, Freud's thinking on the unconscious forces provides us with an understanding that not everything that happens in groups is logical, rational and conscious. However, this is just one perspective, and, as we can see, there are others. For many people, these concepts are very useful to explain some of the inexplicable phenomena that happen in group dynamics, but if they do not 'sit well' with your experiential knowledge framework, it may provide the opportunity to reflect on your reactions.

Behaviourist perspective

The key contributor to thinking about the behaviourist theories on groups is Burrhus Frederic Skinner (1904–1990). His perspective is the exact opposite of Freud's, as he proposed that the unconscious has no part to play at all, and that mental states are not significant. He held that all human activity could be scientifically analysed by observation. In addition, behaviour that is conducive to the well-being of society can be re-enforced through rewards, and negative behaviour can be constrained by punishment (http://psychclassics.yorku.ca/Skinner/Twotypes/twoty-pes.htm, 2008). Skinner reached beyond the classical conditioning of Ivan Pavlov (1849–1936), with ethical considerations. The essential beliefs of behaviourism include the perception that human and animal behaviour are on a continuum, and that much can be learned about human behaviour by observing animal behaviour. For example, famous experiments on animals include the 'Pavlov's Dog' one. This experiment was based on the observation that dogs salivate when they sense food. Pavlov was able to condition a dog to salivate at the sound of a bell, as he had connected the food with the sound of the bell. From this, it was deduced that people's behaviour could be controlled by conditioned reflex, the 'carrot and stick' approach.

Behaviourism is very influential in education and training, in addition to underpinning a psychotherapeutic approach. This includes therapies such as aversion therapy to help people to avoid harmful substances, or desensitization to help people to overcome phobias, like fear of birds or flying. Curriculum development in formal education has based itself on behaviourist models of learning. Objectives and outcomes express changes in people's behaviour. For example, when an objective or outcome relates to the development of skills, they refer to observable behaviour rather than attitudinal changes or consciousness raising. For example:

> At the end of this module, the student will be able to ...
> At the end of this session, students will have acquired the skills of ...

The fundamental critiques of the behaviourist perspectives centre on the wholeness of human experience, simplifying and reducing it into unconnected parts. This is a key contribution from the Gestalt approach, which promotes the much more holistic perspective of human beings. For example, there are many examples of learning that go beyond purely conditioning or conditioned reflex. The use of language is very complex and complicated, yet very young children can correctly use grammar and punctuation, and this usage is regardless of reward. Indeed, many children are 'punished' for the overuse of language, like the endless 'why?' questions of toddlers, by the exasperated parent.

Then there is the issue of people learning from others, again with no reward or punishment, even imaginary others, like characters from novels, television and comics. That is, a person copies the characters, real or imaginary. How many people have played at being the wonderful footballer who scores the winning goal? Or the private detective who solves the crime when everyone else is stumped?

Tennant (1997) provides a useful discussion on the issue of the behaviourist approach in adult learning (pp. 96–106). However, for me, the most compelling argument against the completely behaviourist approach is the fragmentation of learning and the process of learning that is separated from the outcome of learning. In adult and community education, the process is as important as the purpose, and a strictly behaviourist approach would deny this.

However, before we examine the purposes and processes in adult and community education, we need to take a closer look at the humanistic approach.

Humanistic approach

The humanistic approach emerged in the 1950s, arising out of the existential movement, and a synergetic amalgamation of psychoanalysis and behaviourism. Existentialism emerged in the nineteenth century, a philosophy which focused on the meaning of existence. In the 1950s the very influential de Beauvoir ([1943] 1989) and Sartre (1989) shaped it. Autonomy, individual power and meaningful living for the person, as a member of society, characterizes the humanistic approach. A number of principles about humanity, particularly a more holistic view of the human condition are crucial to humanistic perspectives, as is the recognition that humans have awareness, responsibility and social dimensions.

One of the cornerstones in the humanistic approach is Carl Rogers (1902–1987) who, together with Abraham Maslow (1908–1970), founded the person-centred approach of the humanistic tradition. Maslow's key contribution was his 'Hierarchy of Human Needs' (1943) matrix, with the needs for shelter, food, safety and love having to be met before the person can work towards fulfilling their potential, 'self-actualization'. When this hierarchy of needs is combined with Roger's thinking on the person, in counselling (1951) and learning (1983) contexts, the approach is developed. It is based on the idea of the autonomous person, who can develop insight and awareness of their 'self', and bring congruence to their ideal self – who they would like to be – and their real self. Their relations with others are based on being the real self, a relation of equality and meaningfulness. In the context of adult and community education, the participants and the tutor are in a learning process of developing the congruence and working towards Maslow's concept of self-actualization. Tutors require empathy and positive regard for the students in order to create the safety that Maslow identifies. Empathic understanding entails seeing the world from the other's point of view, without getting entangled with it; and unconditional positive regard means not judging them, and being positively disposed towards them.

While both Rogers and Maslow focus completely on the individual, the humanistic approach has developed a social dimension, closely connected with rights, in the context of democracy. The aims of the approach include the self-actualization of the person along with the development of group democracy. Elsewhere, I have discussed this at greater length (Connolly, 1999: 118–121) but the key point that needs to be made here, is that the view of the person in the humanistic approach is a major advance on the idea of the student as a blank slate and the teacher as all-knowing. Again, this is central in adult and community education.

This section endeavoured to provide a brief background to three central influences underpinning groupwork, demonstrating the links with other spheres in society. It is clear that these perspectives have their origins in very traditional views of the family, of class, of community and of society, yet they do provide a guiding light through a very complex maze of human relations. However, it is not necessary to adopt one approach to groupwork and reject the others. Many adult educators have an integrative approach, drawing on newly emerging thinking in human and social studies, and techniques that have developed in other fields. The essential point for adult and community educators is to take into account that people in groups think, feel and behave, and that it is their responsibility to facilitate this. Facilitation skills and styles will be the substance of Chapter 7. But first, the next section will look at the purposes and processes which underline all groupwork in adult and community education.

Purpose and process

From the late 1940s, two distinct functions were identified in groups: the work that had to be done, and the way in which it was done (Benne and Sheats, 1948, cited in Hogan, 2002). These functions were called task and maintenance, implying a fairly mechanistic view of group dynamics. The task of the group is the work that must be undertaken in order to fulfil its aim, while the maintenance is what needs to be done in order to enable the group to fulfil its aim. For example, in my applied arts class, the task of the group was to learn some skills in needlework in order to apply them practically, that is, the content of the class. The maintenance was the way in which the relaxed environment and praise and validation of the tutor gave us the confidence to learn and apply the skills, that is, the style and methods of the tutor.

In adult learning groups, the mechanical model is not appropriate, and the human and social dimensions are not taken into account. In order to take these on board, I find that the terminology 'purposes and processes' of the group is more fitting. I choose these terms because they stem from the ordinary, everyday educational language, generally. For example, a term such as 'aim' is commonplace in adult and community education curricula, and increasingly we see the use of 'learning outcomes' to express the idea that adult and community education is purposeful and focused. In addition, the intentions of adult and community education include both micro and macro goals, personal and social.

The purposes of adult and community education cannot be attained without recourse to ways of working towards them: the processes. These processes include the helpfulness of the tutor, such as praise and interest; the methods they use to impart information; the chat among the participants to help them to understand one another.

The characteristics of the learning group overlap with the characteristics of any group. The key characteristic is that members know they are a group. This seems to be blindingly obvious, but a group is self-conscious, not a random, unknowing collection of people, and members recognize each other as fellow members. Thus, a crowd waiting at a bus stop could develop a group identity if they begin to interact and see themselves as having a common purpose, and as different from the passers-by or the people at another bus stop. In the night class, we began to drift together as we registered and moved towards the room indicated. At that first stage, already we were able to develop some level of process, even if it was just to say we didn't know what we were doing. However, as a group, we knew we were there with an identical purpose, that is, to learn arts and crafts. We knew that we were the group in pursuit of this purpose, and that we had a connection with one another on the basis of the common purpose, and the recognition that we had an identity as the group of students. In addition, as we got to know one another, and commented on our handiwork and on our life stories, we subtly and not so subtly influenced one another. By the time we finished the course, we knew one another very well, and were very sad that we would not meet again. We pledged support to one another, and a few went on to become very good friends. This experience reflects that of many people working with adults in adult and community education.

That is, the first characteristic of the learning group is that each member shares a common purpose of an overt learning event, and each member comes in contact with all the other members as a result of this common purpose. There can be covert purposes, which may emerge in the lifetime of the group, either positively or negatively. The covert purposes can include secret agendas, like a person who needed to get out of the house for sake of her own sanity. A participant could have a covert personal agenda to set up her own business, or have a desire to make a gift for a friend. Indeed, in each group, there is probably a covert purpose for each participant. However, the work of the learning group is to focus on the learning purpose, primarily, while respecting the covert purposes. The work of the individual members is to figure out if their personal or secret purposes are compatible with the learning purpose.

Moreover, there are other levels of covert purposes. The concept of the 'hidden curriculum' is widely critiqued in formal education, especially in Lynch (1989). Lynch draws on neo-Marxist thinking to look at how education exacerbates gender, race and class inequalities (p. xi). The term hidden curriculum was coined in the late 1960s. It expresses how education, as a social institution, reinforces social, racial and gender inequality, thus maintaining the *status quo*. Through the education system the *status quo* is reproduced. Apple, in 1982, maintains that formal education is organized around the needs of the individualized, career-orientated state and economy, which contradicts its overt aim of the redistribution of the wealth and benefits of society (1982: 152–5). A fairly one-dimensional example might be the way the class system is maintained when the needs of working-class children are not met, leading to unhappiness and alienation and early school-leaving, leading to fewer opportunities for participation in society, and bringing about the cycle of educational disadvantage to the children of those early school leavers. Simultaneously, the children of middle-class parents do well in the system adapted to meet their needs, and they could benefit not only from the formal educational system, but also from private supports, leading to greater success in school examinations, more professional opportunities, and emerging at the same level of social status as their parents, or at a higher one. This cycle is replicated in their children, a loop of upward mobility.

Interestingly, the intervention of adult and community education is a key way to break the cycle of educational disadvantage. This perhaps is the keystone of the hidden curriculum of adult and community education. The purpose of adult and community education is to bring about social change, enabling people to participate fully in society as citizens, learners, workers, mothers, fathers and so on.

Purpose of the learning group

In a learning group, the goal of the group is to acquire new skills, knowledge and competences. Every person in the group knows they are there for this purpose, and that everyone else is also on a learning journey. In adult and community education, teaching and learning is the primary task of the group, and this task is what makes it different to other groups. If we look at other groups we know that the task of those groups could and do include learning outcomes, but the learning outcomes are not the primary task. This is the key distinguishing characteristic of the learning group in adult and community education.

The implications of this are manifold. When we look at the developments in adult and community education since the mid-1970s, we can see strong parallels with psychotherapy, self-help and support groups. This has led many people to conclude that there is no real difference between, say, a therapeutic group and a learning group. And many people join in adult and community education to have their needs for therapy met, rather than their learning needs.

When we learn, we change. This is a profound realization, and it explains in some way the confusion that people might experience when they try to locate the learning group in the same category as therapeutic groups. The difference when they compare and contrast learning groups and other groups centres on knowledge. Learning in adult and community education brings a quality of change that builds on our experience, but it goes further than that. It connects our experience with the body of knowledge that is within the learning group, including the tutor's, with a body of knowledge outside of the group and, almost like fertilizer, facilitates its organic growth.

When we participate in a therapeutic group, we can gain insight and awareness into ourselves and into the group, but it is not connecting with a body of knowledge outside of the group. When we participate in a support group, or a self-help group, again we are not connecting with outside knowledge. Rather, it relies on the embodied knowledge of those within the group.

It might be difficult to understand why this is so profound. Historically, adult and community education has challenged canonical knowledge, particularly since the mid-1970s. However, this does not mean that knowledge is discarded: on the contrary, new knowledge is created and recreated in the process of learning, in a continual cycle of renewal. This means that the goal of the learning group is to participate in this cycle, to contribute to the body of knowledge. In addition, the ultimate goal of adult and community education is emancipation, consciousness raising and citizenship, and 'really useful knowledge' is vital to this. Thus, in the creation of new knowledge, the political dimensions are at the forefront, critical knowledge which adds to our understandings of society. This knowledge underpins the skills and competencies which are also the goal of learning groups. When I think about my first experience, the tutor provided the background knowledge to the handicrafts and the skills. For example, she gave an historical account of stitches, of cloth, of patterns; a brief introduction to the social background to women's work, and how it fitted in with the work of the time. At times, we all discussed the role of decoration and aesthetically pleasing household objects, such as embroidered tea towels, and 'good' tablecloths, used only for special occasions. This is a model for all learning groups in adult and community education: the underpinning knowledge is not just about the steps in acquiring the skills, the behavioural changes that will emanate from the skills, or the competence and ease with any particular skill. In adult and community education, the knowledge is the exercise for the mind, the wherewithal to think critically about what we are learning.

The purpose of learning groups is to acquire knowledge, skills and competencies. This is what makes it different to other types of group. But it is not just the purpose that is different, the process is also different.

Process in the learning group

We have seen that the purpose of the learning group has profound implications for the group, and it might be seductive to conclude that while the goal is different, the way the work is carried out is indistinguishable from that of other groups. But it is not the case. Again, there is considerable common ground between the processes of other groups, but there are also strong differences. When we consider again the place of the interaction between people in the group, we immediately grasp that the interaction is central. Otherwise, why be in a group? It would probably be much easier to stay alone, studying material already compiled in books or on the Internet. However, the process in the learning group makes the goal meaningful; it facilitates the learning and enables the learners to engage with the knowledge at a very significant level. Indeed, the process in the learning group ensures that the interaction goes beyond the superficial and enables the members of the group to operate at a deep level.

If I reflect again on the experience of the arts and crafts class, the key difference between the process of adult and community education and mainstream education was the atmosphere. It was imbued by a completely distinct ethos: instead of power and control in the hands of the teacher, or the curriculum, or some other authority, it was in our hands. This meant that the students created the atmosphere with a combination of their expectations of the teacher and the subject; their reasons for registering for the class; and their individual personalities and life experiences.

The medium of process in the learning group is communication, at least at the conscious, overt level. Discussion, dialogue, purposeful conversation, debate, argument, analysis, enquiry, informal talk, exploration, examination: all of these play central roles in the process of the learning group. Assertive, open, direct and forthright communication is the ideal medium. But communication is not just all talk. It must include active listening, the lifeblood of communication, if learning is to take place. Thus, interactivity, interdependence and influence are enabled through good communication.

The key dimension of the process of the learning group is the well-being of the members. This is contingent on a number of factors, but especially the underpinning ethos of the group, and the way in which group members relate to one another. Thus, the overall process of the learning group is concerned with the welfare of the group members, fostering a learning environment in order to distribute the responsibility for the well-being to each member. Ultimately, the process is a shared undertaking for the group.

The purpose and the process in learning groups are interlinked inextricably. The purposes are overtly and clearly tied in with a learning process, and the process is the way in which the learning is conveyed. However, the group dynamic has both the overt dimension, clearly observable and perceptible, and also a covert dimension.

Hidden purposes and processes

As we have already seen, the key legacy of Sigmund Freud to the twentieth century was the role of the unconscious in human relations. For at least 300 years, human development was founded on a set of logical, rational, reasonable and balanced principles. Emotion, in particular, was considered unworthy of the educated, rational man and was largely relegated to the realm of the female. Freud theorized that there was another aspect of humanity that was denied in this rational model, that of the unconscious. This unconscious aspect functioned at the level of the individual, but also at the level of the collective. Society did not progress and develop in a linear, logical, predictable way. Rather, it developed in leaps and troughs. Society unfolded in completely illogical ways, driven by forces that were definitely underneath the surface. This subterranean level is at work in society, and it is also at work in human interactions.

Simultaneously, the way the hidden purpose of a learning group is carried out may also be through the hidden process. These interactive dimensions can completely subvert the overt dimensions, unless the group members become aware of their hidden purposes and processes. The focus on process is a key way for the learning group to uncover the hidden sides of their learning group. Through the process, group members are enabled to bring out what is really happening in the group, especially if the hidden dimensions are preventing them from reaching their goal.

The hidden dimensions stem from a wide range of sources. This section will explore the locations of these hidden dimensions, linking the personal dimensions with the social dimensions.

Social settings

The briefest introduction to sociology shows that a lot goes on in society that is not planned. It goes well beyond the will of the government, and certainly beyond the will of the people. These include the effects from outside the state: in a globalized world, we are affected by global economics, the environment, population migration and so on. Within the state, we are divided socially by class, gender, ethnicity, poverty, disability and many other factors. Part of the process of being a human being in society is to internalize the norms, values and attitudes of that society. These are determined by the most powerful in that society, and they generally reflect the conditions that keep the powerful in power. For further discussion on this, it is rewarding to look at Giddens's *Sociology: A Brief but Critical Introduction* (1986).

In the context of groupwork for adult and community education, many of these hidden social agendas centre around power relations. For most people, their experience in their interactions with the state has been that of authority and subordination. The interaction that most people have had is through the education system or the health system, but the system that controls the physical environment is most pervasive. Roads, buildings, town planning, the built environment, open, public spaces, private spaces: these are the elements in which we live, and yet have very little control over. The interaction of the people with the education system and the health system reinforces this lack of power, and, for many people, it becomes internalized to a greater or lesser degree. This has two effects, at least. One is to accept it all, and defer to the authority, while the other is to fight against it, constantly, using whatever weapons are available. When adult learners bring this into the adult and community education environment, it may have these two effects. The group defers to the tutor, attributing authority to them, that they do not exercise or want to exercise; or the learner will constantly challenge, disrupt and divert the group in their work towards their goal. If adult educators bring this model into the adult and community education environment, they will try to control the group against their wishes, privileging their own authority over that of the group members. The outcome in any case is undemocratic, unequal and unfair. The key underlying purpose of the learning group is to develop democracy and participation, and the key underlying process is to facilitate it. We have looked at 'really useful knowledge' and 'really useful methods' in Chapters 3 and 4. However, this is not the end of the story. As I mentioned earlier, groups develop over their lifetimes, and it is crucial to understand this development, if 'really useful groupwork' is to happen. The next chapter will look at the stages of group development, the third point of the triangle of groupwork theory.

Conclusion

This chapter looked at the key characteristics of learning groups, distinguishing them from other groups. I drew on thinking underpinning groupwork and the purposes and processes that occur in the dynamic interaction within groups, and I endeavoured to critically reflect on the connections between adult and community education and personal and social transformation. It explored the theories drawn from other spheres, and interrogated them in terms of their appropriateness for adults learning in groups. It built on the preceding chapters with regards to integrating 'really useful methods' with the groupwork that developed in both education and the wider society. It continued to review the purpose and process of learning groups, and finally explored the hidden dimensions including the hidden curriculum. In the next chapter, I will further the exploration of development in groups, relating to classical theory, but updating the thinking for the twenty-first century.

Reflection

In your learning journal, consider the following questions:

- Do you think and feel differently when you are in different groups?
- Can you give examples?
- What groupwork perspective do you feel more drawn to?
- Why?
- Can you identify elements of the 'hidden curriculum' in your experience of education?

6   Development in learning groups

Key ideas: classic model of development; growth and development in learning groups; power in learning groups

Introduction

One of my key experiences as an adult learner was in a group of mature, funny, interesting co-learners, who came from a wide variety of backgrounds. One was from a national agency managing forests, while another was a development worker, working in different parts of the world affected by famine. A third was a trainer of people with disabilities, and a fourth taught cookery to prisoners. The age range in the group was from early 20s to late 50s, and women were in the majority. Everything was going well. We found the course a welcome respite from the rest of our lives. Indeed, for me, it was a social outlet, as I had two small children. In common with a lot of parents of small children, it was difficult to have conversations which did not revolve around the needs of the children, and the course was a breather for a few hours a week. In short, it was an interesting and stimulating place to be.

After a number of weeks had passed, a strange mood seeped into the group. People started to get snippy with one another, impatient when some learners spoke, or argumentative with the tutors. Things came to a head with a mini-explosion, in which people expressed their discontent. After the blow-up, people were a bit more cautious, looking at each other a bit more circumspectively. However, things settled down again, and soon, relationships improved and we got on with our learning.

I didn't know anything about stages of development in groups at that time, but I was intrigued about how the darker mood seeped into the group. It was quite different to the fights in families in two key ways. The participants were still on good behaviour with none of the storming around, sarcasm or personal attacks that would be more typical of people in close relationships. On the other hand, the group did not agree on the cause of the dark mood. Some felt it was due to the tutor who did not control a talkative person. Others felt it was the talkative person who had no idea how they were affecting the group, while yet others felt that anyone who was complaining had no tolerance, and they should just put up with it. I'm sure that there were many other views, but the thing for me was the diversity of the perspectives.

When I actually studied the stages of group development, this made more sense to me. I was not afraid of conflict, but I did think it was destructive. And I had believed that reasonable, mature people were not prey to collective moods, and did not need to have conflict. They could reconcile their differences in many ways besides conflict. That has all changed for me now, though, and this is the most significant shift for me in my work in adult and community education. I do not go out of my way to bring on conflict, but I see it, handled well, as enriching and progressive and a catalyst for change.

When I reflect on my experience in the group as a learner, I realize that people, including myself, needed a clearer route to self-expression, and the conflict provided the opportunity to open up the level of honesty in the group. Although many years have passed, when I speak to my fellow learners, we always refer back to that time. This is an indication of how significant it was as a collective experience. It was a learning opportunity that was well worthwhile, by any reckoning.

It is inherently human to grow and develop throughout life, and it always signals health and well-being when people actively pursue stimulating environments in which their minds and bodies are engaged and challenged. We mark off the stages of development for children, seeing each stage as an accomplishment. Increasingly, adults experience stages of development, and these do not stop at the age of 50 or 60 or whatever. One of the most rewarding aspects of adult education is the encounter with older people, who embody wisdom and experience from which everyone else can learn. Simultaneously, they can learn from younger people, who contribute fresh ways of looking at the world. However, this is by way of introduction to the development in learning groups, congruent with the rest of human development and just as complicated. This chapter will look at the classical models of development, and explore them in relation to the newer perspective drawn from the experience of working in social movement, community and learning groups. Groups are constantly changing and developing, in line with the human condition. Classical theory conceptualized this as the stages of development, but thinking in more recent times has characterized these developmental stages as fragmented and multifaceted.

However, it is vital to acknowledge that we all need some stability and consistency. Without it, life would be chaotic and practically impossible to manage. Stability and consistency are like the cardinal points of the compass. They do not tell us where to go. Rather, they guide us as we make our journey in the world. Change is the constant travelling companion on that journey.

I will look at the classical model of development, before continuing to the elements that influence thinking more recently, drawing on accounts of human development, community development and social progress.

Stages of group development

Bruce Tuckman devised the famous stages of group development in the mid-1960s, (Tuckman, 1965). Thinking about group development followed thinking about life span development, which highlighted the milestones that people attained as they matured. These included physical milestones, like puberty and social development, such as playing cooperatively with friends; and learning milestones, like reading age. It is easy to see that these milestones signal optimistic and progressive advancements and that they act as a metaphor for all facets of development. Although I cannot read Tuckman's mind, his stages of group development echo the life span milestones. He coined the 'forming, storming, norming and performing' rhyming mnemonic, revisiting it in 1977 and adding 'adjourning', in an attempt to capture the milestones in the life of groups.

These terms endeavour to capture the energy of movement, progress, regress and resolution in the life of groups. The development of groups is crucial in order to arrive at the optimal stage for work. In addition, the system of the group is parallel to the development of the individuals within the group. Further, this scheme emphasizes the importance of conflict – storming – as a developmental stage. And conflict seems to be the most difficult aspect of groupwork, with a negative connotation that is either denied or allowed to tear the group apart. This section will look at this classical model in more detail, and suggest a further revision, in the light of the changes since the mid-1970s.

Developing values

Thinking about development is crucially significant in order to connect with the experience of groups, rather than looking at them as a kind of distant, objective observer. In our interaction with other members of society, when we think of ourselves as active, engaged and interested in others, we can journey alongside them, enriching everyone. Studying groupwork could leave us like scientists looking through a microscope, at this strange phenomenon on the specimen slide. This is particularly true when considering the stages of group development. There is a sense that group development is beyond the control of members, and it is inevitable, like organic growth on the one hand, and the negative trials and tribulations of life, on the other. In addition, there is a sense that members of the group are at the mercy of 'difficult' people, who can disrupt the work with their unmanageable behaviour. Thinking reflectively about the stages of group development can help us to look at the entity of the group, and our own contribution to it, as well as looking at the effect of others on us. Briefly, though, I want to outline the classical model, and connect it with the experience of being a group member.

Forming

Probably, everyone has had the experience of going into a crowded room at one time or another, and looking anxiously around for someone we can identify or identify with. This may be a social event, a meeting, a party or a class. The forming stage is that stage of acute awareness, when we look at one another and try to discern if we are in the right place. We try to distinguish who the others are and establish some kind of common ground. We hold onto our courage as we fathom why we are here and start identifying others as types with whom we can connect. Hopefully, at this stage in a learning group, the tutor comes in with good humour and reassures us all that we are welcome, and that they are looking forward to working with us.

The forming stage can be a very anxious one. People are out of their normal environment and the unknown looms ominously. This can be the case even if the potential participants are fully aware of what they have signed up for and even if they have a lot of experience of new groups. The tentative nature of the experience is unsettling, especially if the person has low confidence and esteem.

When we look at this stage more closely, we can see that it is like the old proverb: 'The longest journey starts with the first step'. This is the first step, and it deeply affects all other steps. Our prior experience is the only thing we can hold onto at the forming stage, and our model for being in the world is our only guide. When we look around for types we can connect with, we often choose people from our own peer group, like people our own age, appearance and gender. She may be glamorous, or he may be earthy. The essential thing is that we are making judgements based on what we think is the case, and this may change considerably as the group progresses. However, while we try to identify fellow travellers, as it were, we are also trying to insert ourselves, to create our place in the new group. Thus, in the short time it takes to form, the group is laying down the foundation of the future development. If the group forms well, the next stage is easier to negotiate.

Storming

When we look at the changes that have taken place globally since the mid-1970s, we have seen fundamental ideological transformations. Some revolutions were 'velvet' revolutions, a grass roots uprising which overthrew very powerful forces, dismantling the USSR, and the old Iron Curtain. Not all of the revolutions were free of violence: the states of the former Yugoslavia waged horrific wars in the immediate aftermath of the fall of the tyrannical dictatorships of the USSR and its satellites. In Ireland, the mid-1990s saw the IRA cessation of violence, followed by the Good Friday Peace Agreement. However, in many other places, violence has increased and worsened, deepening the conflicts that divide states and peoples. That is, change is contingent on the challenge to the *status quo*. How that is handled is not just important for interpersonal relations, but for the good of humankind. Of all the purposes of groupwork, managing difference is probably the most important. Groupwork is trying to model ways of managing conflict in the most beneficial ways, beneficial to the members and beneficial to the wider community and society. Groupwork in adult learning groups also ensures that difficulties among group members, or between group members and the tutor, are managed in order to enhance the group. This resonates with my experience in the learning group, when conflict erupted, but the result was improved working relations with all concerned though, it could also have been destructive. However, according to Tuckman, the storming stage is the prelude to the next, the norming stage.

Norming

According to Tuckman, this stage refers to the establishment of overt or covert principles for working together. This is the stage when the culture of the group is laid down and the values, attitudes and perspectives take a collective flavour, rather than individualized qualities. That is, individuals may still hold stances that are at variance with the group, but the prevailing norms predominate.

The group members identify more closely with the group and, simultaneously, assert their autonomy. The task of the group is to become more fully engaged with the group, and to attend to interpersonal relationships. This is parallel to norms in any grouping, like a community or a region, or, indeed, religious, ethnic and cultural groups. The identity of the grouping links to the norms and the grouping upholds it in different ways. These ways include the overt or covert inclusion and exclusion of members and potential members. I had the misfortune to join a sports club with my children, and although I did everything that I was supposed to do on the surface, below the surface they did not want either the children or me. One or two of the club welcomed me, but they were not able to overcome the predominant norms. I still do not know what those norms were, but I do know that they squeezed out my family. I could have left it at that, until exactly the same thing happened to another family.

This can happen in learning groups, particularly groups who have a relationship with one another, like a group that has progressed from one year to the next, with some new members. Again, it is the tutor's work to address it, in order to include the new people, and create a new norm for the group. The creation of the norms, according to Tuckman, is prior to the next stage, *performing.*

Performing

This is the stage of development when the group get most of the real work done. People are working together in an effective way. The norming stage establishes equality and fairness, if that is clearly on the agenda of the learning group, where all members are equal in power and influence. They realize that interpersonal relationships form part of the success of the group, and they balance the relationships and the work of the group. Members develop their sense of themselves as individuals and as belonging to the group; they engage in high quality discussion and they develop deeper meanings in their experience. The timetable dictates the duration of the performing stage, and this creates the endgame towards which the members work. This leads to the final stage, the *adjourning* stage.

Adjourning

This is the end stage, when the group disbands. Many people who have had good experiences with their group want to continue meeting, either in a learning or other social capacity. They organize reunions and celebrate anniversaries. In any event, members will probably experience a sense of loss when the group comes to an end, giving rise to the alternative label for this stage, the *mourning* stage. However, once the work of the group is over, it's over. If the course or programme continues to another year or level, a new group forms to fulfil the new objectives.

Critical reflection

This famous five was very influential when it was published in the 1960s and 1970s, and it probably interpreted a sense that people had that their experience in groups was not static. At the very least, people felt closer to other group members, and the synergy of the dynamics helped people to have a sense of achievement. However, while the model is a very good introduction to developmental processes in groupwork, the model is not up to the task of analysing deeply what is really going on in groups. The key problem with it is the problem that I have raised consistently in this book: that human, community and social development does not progress along linear pathways, in sequential order. It is much messier than that. Moreover, while a group culture emerges, this does not mean that the group members are homogeneous, and further, it is no guarantee that this enhances their cooperation and collaboration. Furthermore, the facilitator has explicit responsibilities to help people to make the most of the learning environment. Finally, and the most important of all, is that conflict can happen at any stage of the group's work, and the absence of conflict is no inhibition to work, either.

I want to discuss this in greater detail, to connect the complexity of group membership, to connect with power distribution in the group and wider society, and to connect with the learning society.

Complexity

Learning groups are highly complex. If I had to nominate stages of learning group development, the only stages that I could say for certain, are the beginning and the end. I know that they begin when people convene at the beginning of the course, and they end when the course is over. People build relationships with one another, depending on trust, openness, taking responsibility and doing the work. Many issues cause conflict in groups, but just as we understand that conflict is typical rather than unusual in the lifeworld, we can deal with it constructively in groups. However, adult educators have the responsibility for helping the group to develop, in terms of learning, and the practice of building a good process is sensitive to how well the people know one another. Thus, rather than look at the stages of group development as if the people found themselves marooned on a desert island, with an unknown observer monitoring them as if they were laboratory experiments, it is more helpful to look at the development in terms of relationships. As Deborah Kerr might have sung in 'The King and I', 'it's about getting to know you, getting to know all about you'. The adult educator has specific responsibility to help the group to achieve just that.

Whether people convene for formal or non-formal educational purposes, they come from a wide variety of backgrounds, and in addition they have a wide variety of expectations and purposes. This means that when they gather they bring that diversity with them. Further, in learning groups there are at least three, and maybe four entities getting together: the individual, the group, the facilitator and even the community of practice to which they belong. Each of these entities has different learning needs and responsibilities. The individuals have their own learning needs, and the group has collective learning needs, which, hopefully, are compatible, but may not be. The facilitator's responsibility is to clarify what needs the learning pro-gramme and the learning group can meet, and what needs they cannot. In addition, the community may need the learners to acquire certain skills and knowledge and this is added in the mix. That is, the learning group makes particular demands on the adult educators. The individuals may not clearly understand these demands, but adult educators need to understand that their responsibilities go beyond providing inputs and facilitating discussions. Their responsibilities extend to helping the group to create an ethical and respectful learning environment. The next section will identify a series of tasks that the adult educator is responsible for, in order to create a good learning environment, while simulta-neously taking care of the overall learning outcomes.

Adult educator group-centred tasks

The group-centred task of the adult educator, at the beginning stage, is to help the group to discover mutually rewarding ways of working, and to clarify their purpose. In addition, the facilitator conveys the values underpinning emancipatory adult learning, and helps the group to engage with it. The activities in Chapter 9 exemplify how the adult educator can carry out this task.

The principles underpinning the learning group, such as respect and tolerance, help to shape the culture. Again, the adult educator has to convey this to the group if the group does not identify this for themselves. And the facilitator reminds the group of these norms if they start to undermine them for any reason.

Perhaps one of the most important tasks the adult educator has in the formation of the learning group is to help them to uncover the hidden aspects of the groups. As we saw when we reviewed the formation of groupwork and critical education, the hidden aspects of the individual learner, the knowledge base and the role in society are there to be uncovered, to a greater or lesser extent. The task of the educator is not to coerce the group. Rather it is to equip them to uncover these themselves through critical reflection.

As the learning group works through the course, adult educators' responsibilities centre on the learning needs, that is, inputs, discussion, creative activities and so on, that enable the group to achieve their goals. They underpin this with reflection and evaluations, such as checking in with the group.

In the duration of the group's life, the adult educator needs to facilitate conflict management, setting aside time to handle it appropriately. There are activities and experiences in Chapter 9 that could be adapted to suit the group.

The group-centred task at the end of the course is to close the learning group in a satisfactory manner. This entails helping them to reflect on their overall learning experience, engaging them in the critical evaluation of how they have changed, what has happened to their values and attitudes and what they have learned, from the course and from one another.

These are learner-centred tasks that guide the group to their learning objectives. There is another aspect of group-centred work that the adult educator needs to attend to in order to ensure that the medium and the message are congruent: the question of power.

Power dimensions and group development

Empowerment is a key outcome of adult learning in groups. The overt aim of learning, knowledge, attitudes, values, methods and facilitation is to redistribute power, to enable people to take control over their own lives. There is a difference between *power over*, which entails exercising power over another, and *power to*, which entails being equipped to have control over one's own life. Power manifests itself in at least three ways (Lukes, 2005). The first is straightforward coercion, which most people can recognize, even if they do not have the wherewithal to withstand it. The second dimension is taking control over the agenda, for example, obstructing decision making. And the third dimension is the most insidious, which is the way power works in a society like the UK and Northern Ireland, where the powerful shape people's mindsets and attitudes, controlling what they think and feel. Adult educators need to work against power over people, obviously, preventing coercion and ensuring the course or programme is not hijacked by funders, vested interests or group members. Adult educators also need to facilitate the members to gain the power to control their own lives, in order to counter the first two dimensions, but, in addition, to equip them to analyse their mindsets and attitudes and develop an authentic set of values, free from propaganda or misinformation. To do this, adult educators need to be aware of the ways in which power is reflected in the group and the ways in which they exercise power themselves. The analysis of power relations is crucial for the healthy functioning of the learning group.

When the individuals convene for the learning group, they bring their social power with them. That is, their status in the lifeworld will determine to some degree how they relate to others in the group. This status might emanate from their occupation, their place in their families, their gender, ethnicity or colour, their experience, their age and so on. For example, the group may listen to a man with more attention than to a woman. The eldest in the family may be a bit bossy, treating the other members of the group like children. A senior citizen may dismiss the opinions of a younger person, or the other way around, just because of their assumptions about age. Overall, these dimensions of power have a deep impact on the working of the group, but even if they do not inhibit the work, they subvert the principle of equality and fairness. Again, adult educators must take responsibility in the early stages of the group, in order that no one exercises power over another.

As the group proceeds towards its goal, quite often these power dimensions arise to challenge the facilitator or other group members. This is a key cause of conflict, rather than any difference of opinion or niggles with another group member.

However, the most important task for adult educators in relation to power dimensions in the group development is to look at their own exercise of power. Obviously, adult educators are human and prone to human frailty, like anyone else. But reflections on the issue of power can help to overcome any default mechanism that leads us to want to control others. A crucial difference between mainstream education and adult and community education is precisely on this point. Teachers, lecturers, and the like, focus a lot on keeping control over the learners. As I said in the first chapter, adult educators work on the basis that the learners are there because they want to be, and they do not need to control them. Thus, if adult educators focus on controlling the group, they need to revisit the motivation of the learners. If the learners do not want to be there, then, they should invite them to leave. Adult learning groups are not the place for incarceration, or a repeat of the traditional classroom.

Conclusion

Tuckman's famous five stages of group development provide a useful insight into the progression of groups as they work towards their goals, but cannot encompass the complexity of human interactions in relationships. This chapter makes the case for the development of relationships, as an essential process in facilitating people's learning. Relationships guard against the abuse of power, and also mitigate the entirely human condition of frailty. The chapter explored the role that the adult educators play in guiding the group through the process of working towards their goals. It looked at the dimensions of power at play in that process, and connected that with the overall objectives of adult education for emancipation.

Reflection

Think of any group that you belong to, regardless of the purpose. Identify how the group moved towards the goal. Reflect on what part the facilitator, leader, chair, educator or whatever played in that. Ask yourself if they made it better or worse, and try to think why. Finally, think of the way power was distributed. Was it fair to you or others in the group?

---

7   Facilitation qualities

Key ideas: facilitation skills and styles; democratic, anti-authoritarian process; application to adult learning groups

Introduction

When I went into my first Women's Studies class as an adult educator, I had only my experience of being a learner or a student to guide me about what to do, as well as what not to do. The context in which I heard the word 'facilitator' was a particularly poisonous one, which depicted the facilitator as a puppeteer, with a helpless marionette dangling at the end of the strings. But it is worth reviewing this context in the light of how facilitation skills have developed since, and the role that facilitation plays in twenty-first century society, in all sorts of contexts, from the furthering the peace process in Northern Ireland to enabling creativity in the workplace. This chapter will explore the development of the qualities of facilitation, and link these qualities to the transformative thinking on citizenship and autonomy, together with the collectivity of cooperation, collaboration and teamwork that characterizes social relationships. As with groupwork in general the principles underpinning facilitation stem from psychotherapeutic thinking, critical citizenship and community development as well as adult and community education, which I have discussed in earlier chapters. I want to narrow the focus to the approach and skills involved in facilitating people in adult learning groups, drawing on thinking that developed in other areas in human and community development. In particular, I want to explore the work of Heron, who has been a primary inspiration for my understanding of the principles of facilitation. Group facilitation is a method of enabling a group of people to work towards their common purpose or goal. This method encourages people to take control of their own needs, and to work collectively towards meeting them. A group is more robust than individuals and has resources, which, when shared, empower partici-pants. In particular, facilitation addresses issues of power, and seeks to enable participants to exercise power in a just way. Facilitation consists of a set of qualities including skills, attitudes, knowledge, approaches and styles, which apply the method of enabling people to work collectively, towards the learning goal, with due attention to power and equality in carrying out the work. Facilitation is ultimately a tool for democracy and in the adult and community education context, the skills provide the tangible link between learning and citizenship. Facilitators work in adult and community education, in lifelong learning, in psychotherapy, in life-coaching, in youth work, as well as peace making and community development, and in many other contexts. In adult and community education, the person who is responsible for initiating teaching and learning, for the learning environment, for the goal and the relationship, is ultimately the tutors who provide multi-dimensions to the task and process, including tutoring, lecturing and facilitating. What is required of this person is not just to be knowledgeable about the subject, but also to create the environment whereby those who have come together can learn, grow and develop. The facilitator in adult and community education has different responsibilities to a facilitator of a therapeutic group, a community development group, or any other type of group. The next section will look at the beginnings of facilitation, before going on to examine the skills and styles that combine with personal approaches to create facilitation qualities.

Beginnings

To contextualize facilitation, it is valuable to revisit the time when it was a relatively unknown concept. My first conscious recollection of the term was at a time of tremendous change in Ireland. The late 1970s and early 1980s witnessed women's community education as it was just about getting off the ground, parallel to the development of adult education initiatives in literacy, in particular. A number of feminist agencies were consolidating their positions, such as the Well Woman Centre, for women's health, Women's Aid, an incisive and needful response to domestic violence, and the Rape Crisis Centres, enabling people to deal with the devastation of sexual assault. These feminist initiatives were strongly group-led, and they advocated group processes as a response to the difficult issues that they addressed. In addition, peace groups working for change in Northern Ireland also looked to group processes to make progress, while community development and adult education were hugely important responses to alienation and oppression in many working-class areas. All sorts of residents' associations, rural associations and so on, were springing up among people generally. That is, people organizing in groups were gaining in popularity and proliferating.

Alongside the community of groups, there was also a huge increase in human growth type of groups. Counselling was becoming the key response for all kinds of personal difficulties, like marriage breakdown, domestic violence, rape and sexual assault, and substance misuse and addictions. With counselling and psychotherapy came the notion of enabling people to work through their problems, a substantial shift from the 'agony aunt' model or the medical model, where an authority, specialist or elite professional would tell the client what to do.

As with many new ideas and practices, not to mention jargon, traditionalists greeted the idea of enabling and facilitating people with a degree of suspicion and guardedness. Traditionalist thinkers include some elite professionals, certainly, but also public figures of all kinds, from academics to political and interest group leaders. For example, in Ireland, religious leaders had a prominent role in public life, and were more likely to rely on traditional authority. In any event, many traditionalists certainly perceived facilitation as a process that could open people to manipulation and deception, and they were very critical of facilitators. The message was a very ominous one. The implication of this depiction was that facilitators duped people into a state of unquestioning acquiescence, fulfilling the hidden agenda of the facilitators. In many ways, the traditionalists were voicing a credible reservation. The power of hidden manipulation was, and still is, a major pressure in society. The role of the elite professionals and specialists is, in part, to bring an expertise based on study and research, and which can withstand the onslaught of the misleading interest groups.

The part that misleading interest groups play in society is unmistakable. Hidden manipulation ranges from subtle messages in advertisements, to the recently coined 'spin', which twists stories to convey a message with the intention of influencing the way people feel and think about them. The proof of the power of advertising is clearly shown by the amount of money that is spent on it, and the shift away from the early informative notices, to the more pervasive and ubiquitous part that it has in everyday life. It would almost be impossible to avoid an advertisement in any human activity that is normal now, from TV to billboards. Yet, provided advertisements are not misleading or objectionable on the grounds of taste, very little attention is given to their effect on the public good. Further, the cult-like groups, which I discussed in Chapter 2, shaped the overall impression that charismatic and convincing leaders or facilitators could manipulate vulnerable people. There was a lack of clarity around the difference between these types of leaders and facilitators, which resulted in the suspicion that facilitators were able to deceive group members in the same way. Thus, in the early stages, the unknown dimensions of groupwork and facilitation were regarded with suspicion.

However, facilitation has gained momentum regardless of this suspicion, as I will discuss in the next section. I then consider the prerequisites for facilitators conveying facilitation qualities.

Critical reflection and facilitation

Critical reflection is an essential tool for countering the hidden agendas of misleading messages. Facilitation is a key way of helping people to develop the critical skills needed. In addition, facilitation helps to counter traditional hierarchical models of authority and subservience. Facilitation aims to empower people. This necessarily entails interfering with the relationship between unquestioned authority and unquestioned subordination. The main point is to facilitate people to become autonomous and independent. Thus, adult and community educators incorporate facilitation skills into their practice. It is vital to recognize that facilitation is not an absence of direction and expertise or a chaotic melée, leaving people to their own devices. Rather, it is a highly organized, critically reflective, skill-based process that depends on the approach and expertise of the facilitators, and underpinning principles of respect, tolerance, trust and transparency. The next section will look at the elements of the approach required for the process, and then look at the skills.

Personal approaches

It is worth the difficulty involved in separating the approach of the facilitators from the skills it takes to carry out the work. When I use this term, approach, I am trying to capture the predispositions of facilitators, which are quite apart from the techniques and skills of facilitation. In other words, facilitation comes from the predilection for justice, fairness and a positive world-view, combined with an optimistic view of the person as a valuable, worthy member of society in their own right, regardless of their social status.

The approach of facilitators is congruent with the principles of emancipatory groupwork. Specifically, this approach is a synergy of self-awareness, their consciousness of social forces, the capacity for identifying with group members and commitment to the process. This approach is contingent on the capacity for reflexivity. By reflexivity, I mean that I reflect, not just on incidences and events, but that I embed this reflection with my own values and beliefs. For example, I was working with a community group, and one of the group members seemed to be unhappy with the process. As I started a round of introductions, he challenged this vociferously. He did not want to spend time on this as he already knew everyone there. He felt that if I wanted to get to know the group, I should do it on my own time, and not waste the group's time.

This was profound. He was right in his assertion that I was the outsider, and the group worked together outside of this particular process. My immediate reaction was that a round of introductions was the 'right' way to start the process, and that he was wrong. At the time, though, I let it go, and started with the learning session asking the group to introduce themselves at a later stage, when they broke into small groups.

When I thought about this afterwards, I acknowledged that the challenge wounded me. I felt that there was a strong element of misogyny in the incident. The participant was able to act in this way because I am a woman. But when I reflected further, I put myself in his shoes. He was unemployed and was using his time in a valuable way, by taking a course, but with no guarantee that he would end up with a job. His contribution to his community was enormous, but not truly recognized and it was unpaid. In short, he brought a history into the learning group, which came out in this challenge to me not to waste his time. Further, as the facilitator, I was on his side. I wanted to make his time in the group as worthwhile as possible. And there are many ways to attend to the processes in the group, which I was able to use, while taking his needs into account. Thus, on reflection, I moved from the immediate reaction that he was just a misogynist, who did not want to be told what to do by a woman, to trying to meet his needs for a good use of time, while ensuring that the group needs were met. Further, even if he was a misogynist, which is not acceptable at all, but especially in a group dedicated to inclusion and development, by treating his challenge with respect and tolerance, I diffused a potential contentious flash point, and he, the rest of the group and myself as the facilitator were able to proceed towards our goal. At the end of the course, this participant was able to acknowledge that it was important to get to know the other group members in a different way, in order to make their community work more effective.

There was a further follow-up to this incident. As the group worked together and developed trust and cooperation, one group member recalled the incident. She said that she was ashamed that she did not speak up at the time. She had felt too shy and intimidated. As a result, she developed the courage to talk about it. In addition, she predicted that, if the same thing were to happen again, she would have the confidence to discuss it, in the group, at the very least. In this one event, there were layers of learning: I was able to do the introductions in a more creative way, appropriate to the group needs; he was able to see how important the process of building the group was; and she was able to find her voice with conviction and commitment. All of these layers of learning depended on reflexivity. This experience was salutary, and helped me to develop greater insight into the facilitative process. However, while the attitude is the most important aspect of working with learning groups, facilitation is also a set of skills, which helps to implement the attitude in practice. John Heron provides a really useful way of thinking about the connections between attitudes and skills. So, before going on to look at skills, I want to turn to Heron's six-categories analysis of facilitation styles.

Facilitation styles

John Heron (1990) has contributed immeasurably to my understanding of facilitation. My impression at first was that facilitation was a static positioning vis-à-vis learners, depending on a fluid, flexible, easy way of being. Heron pointed out that, rather than being static, facilitators must adapt their style according to what the group needs. In the beginning, people may need a lot of direction, in order to feel secure, while at times of high tension they may need a cathartic intervention. On the other hand, when a group is well on its way it does not need a lot of direction from the facilitator and does not need a very dramatic presence. Facilitators have to find their own styles, of course, but Heron's work illuminates the set of spectra, and facilitators must reflect on where they should be on those spectra, in their unfolding relationship with group members.

These are the categories, expressed as qualities at opposite ends of the spectrum. Facilitators can use these categories to reflect on their current practice, and to consider what they ought to do in order to meet the needs of the group.

Directive/non-directive

The facilitator decides how much direction the group needs, how much information and what instructions in order to meet its targets. In the beginning of the life of the group, at the getting started stage, it needs more direction from the facilitator, while as it goes through the stages of development the facilitator moves to a more non-directive style.

Delegation/non-delegation

The facilitator starts off by not delegating functions and tasks to members of the group and gradually delegates most of the tasks and a large proportion of the maintenance to the group members, when the facilitator is satisfied that they can adhere to the group contract and have established that they are self-motivating.

Delegation is vital for a facilitator, especially when the workload increases. To be able to delegate is a delicate process, but worth practising. Delegation is also important to the development of leadership skills in the group, when members can be entrusted with the well-being of the members.

Interpretative/non-interpretative

The facilitator explores the meaning of dialogue, conversation and inputs. They do this interpreting by paraphrasing or suggesting alternative suitable words to participants.

An interpretative style is especially important in the early life of the group and in active listening. It is also important when issues such as accent and articulation arise. The facilitator checks out what the speaker has said, to clarify for the group. As the group moves on, the facilitator steps back, so that the group interpret for themselves, while remaining in touch to clarify or to deal with any problems that may emerge.

Cathartic/non-cathartic

This aspect of facilitation styles centres on the facility of allowing the cathartic release of pent-up emotion of the members through shouting, crying or laughing.

Some facilitators may feel that catharsis has no place in a learning group. However, groups do experience tension, conflict and other difficulties, and it is vital to be able to look after that. But as the spectrum implies, the facilitator has to make a judgement call as to when it is appropriate and when it is not.

Structuring/non-structuring

Some facilitators are extremely structured with regards to timetables, length of contributions, the organization of materials and so on, while others do not seem to have any structure at all, just turning up and letting the class happen. These two approaches are not always the best for the well-being of the group. Some level of structure is important, as is some level of fluidity and flexibility. The facilitator has to judge when to shift along this spectrum, when to have a high level of structure, and when to let it go. It is always important to be fully prepared, obviously.

Disclosing/non-disclosing

Many facilitators use their own experiences as tools for learning and development in a group, as bell hooks does (1994) and I do myself. Others guard their privacy. The approach adopted by the facilitator will influence the way the group discloses personal details. It is appropriate for some level of disclosure to occur in most groups, especially when the content touches on their lives. However, some people will use the group in a quasi-therapeutic way (see the self-confessor) and the facilitator will have to be aware of the boundaries and have ground rules to deal with this.

This has given overview of Heron's work on facilitation styles, which help to prepare the foundation for the skills required for effective, healthy learning group functioning. The next section will continue with an exploration of the skills involved.

Facilitation skills

Certain qualities are important in the skills, knowledge, ability, styles and approaches involved in facilitation. A good facilitator embodies the entire history of human development, the political shifts that have brought democracy, human rights and social justice to this moment. Because facilitation is ultimately a catalyst for democracy it is crucial for the facilitator to have an awareness of social relationships, that is, the way power, exclusion and marginalization operate in society. They also have to have the skills to deal with the implications of these social relationships.

Facilitation skills centre on those of communication, especially listening and speaking assertively. Skilled facilitators bring together systematic skills with the philosophy that underpins their work and personal approach, all of which add up to a set of qualities which characterizes facilitation. The skills of facilitation include: the ability to listen, assertive communication, self-awareness, raised consciousness, empathy, respect, tolerance, critical thinking, flexibility, a sense of boundaries, the ability to design and implement a learning programme/ session/seminar, etc. for a group, and the ability to evaluate, summarize and plan.

The ability to listen

Listening involves absorbing what participants say and letting them know they are heard. It means decoding language, interpreting non-verbal messages as well as what is being said, and clarifying ambiguous messages. It has two aspects or components: non-verbal and verbal.

Non-verbal listening requires that facilitators be acutely aware of their body language. Eye contact is essential and they need to be aware if they are becoming glazed or dazed looking. They should be careful that their facial expression is empathetic and they are facing the speaker in a relaxed and open way, respecting the speaker's personal space.

Verbal listening sounds like a contradiction but it specifically addresses the problems with articulation and the feeling of being misunderstood. Verbal listening involves clarifying what the person has said by paraphrasing; summarizing, drawing together the strands of thought expressed by the speaker; reflecting back to the person that the facilitator has understood the content of what is said and the emotion of the speaker; encouraging the speaker; and using open-ended questions to move the speaker on and to draw him/her out.

Assertiveness

Assertiveness is the skill of interpersonal relating in an open, direct and honest way. It is underpinned by the principle of equality. It involves a genuine respect for other people and for oneself. In assertive expression, the facilitator models a method of communication which ensures that discussions and other processes are conducted in a safe way for the members of the group. Above all, it isolates aggressive and manipulative behaviour and indicates the inappropriateness of such behaviour in group skills. Assertiveness is a personal skill that is fundamental to effective groupwork. It entails that facilitators and groups members have to take full responsibility for what they say and feel. It ensures that an atmosphere of mutual respect is created and that the ground rule of listening and responsibility is implemented.

Assertive communication is essential for handling difficult situations. In assertive communication, difficult situations can be approached and named in an open way and put to the group for resolution. For example, if a member attempts to dominate, the facilitator could say to the dominant person:

> 'I find it difficult to make sure other people participate, in the limited time available.'
> 'I feel that this group is not progressing when the topics/issues are not relevant.'

'I think that there is a lack of respect for other members of the group.'
'I feel that a rigid positioning stops people listening to other points of view.'

Assertive communication is a multi-dimension tool located in the personal and the social worlds. As a personal attribute, it builds self-respect and esteem, and can enhance confidence and personal development. As a tool for interpersonal relationships, it creates clarity, openness and directivity. Finally, it is probably the most important skill for modern life, as it carries with it the ideals of twenty-first century democratic and egalitarian principles.

Self-awareness

Facilitators need to be acutely aware of themselves, to know their inner landscape (Palmer, 1998), to know what they think and feel and why. They have to develop the capacity to evaluate their own qualities, skills and practice. They need to be honest in their evaluation, and that honesty in acknowledging their limitations will set a tone for authenticity for the entire group. In this context, authenticity is not the same as complete disclosure: rather it is a deep personal awareness, combined with clearly set boundaries.

Critical consciousness

Consciousness as a concept is highly controversial (Blackmore, 2005). However, in this context is it related to self-awareness, but focused on the world outside – the social landscape of predominant ideas. Critical consciousness is the capacity to perceive and understand the forces operating in society, creating inequality, unfairness and marginalization. It begins with a moment of deep revelation when we see a familiar experience, entity or action in a completely different way, a way that transforms our perception.

Critical thinking

This is the capacity to analyse, to go beyond simple, obvious responses to information. It develops understanding by looking for evidence, and by clarifying theories and concepts. It involves looking at underpinning assumptions, looking for alternative explanations and searching for reasons that are more complex. It avoids spurious emotive hooks that blur judgement and false, misleading arguments.

Empathy

Empathy is the ability to sense what other people are feeling and experiencing and to relay that sense back to them. This is perhaps the most essential quality in facilitation, and it ensures that the facilitator really does understand the world from other people's perspectives. Mirroring is a useful technique as it constantly checks for understanding with the other person or members of the group. However, empathy does not mean imagining what the other is thinking in the absence of evidence, rather it connects to the other person's world, not their own inner world.

Respect

This ability ensures that the group members acknowledge each others' rights and do not engage in activities or behaviours that might undermine other participants.

Tolerance

Tolerance is the capacity to accept others as they are when you disagree with them, profoundly or superficially, provided their beliefs and values are able to co-exist with democratic and human rights values. It goes beyond powerless resignation, and it accommodates diversity and difference.

Flexibility

Adopting a strong position and refusing to consider other options is anathema to good facilitation. This does not mean that the facilitator should not have personal beliefs, but it does entail that others' views and beliefs are respected. The facilitator shows flexibility by refusing to be dogmatic or rigidly authoritarian.

Boundaries

A boundary is the division of various aspects of work within groups and between groupwork and personal life. Boundaries will enable participants to be clear about the goals of the learning group, what is appropriate in the group and what is expected of each participant. Boundaries will probably vary in the life of the group, for example, touch may be completely taboo in the early stages while it may be vital at the closing stage. It is up to the facilitators to achieve consensus around boundaries and to use their own judgment about the limits to be set. Poor boundaries will almost certainly result in the group losing its way, the participants feeling alienated and distressed. Boundaries have to be included in the group grounding principles, or group commitment validation.

The ability to evaluate and summarize

These skills develop alongside active listening, combining with the facilitator's own capacity to judge in a larger context. This ability is vital to enable the group to view and reflect on its own work and process from another perspective.

The ability to design and implement learning for a group

The facilitator will draw out the elements of the learning needs of the group, pooling their own knowledge and experience with that of the group. The facilitator endeavours to compile the expressed needs of the group into a framework and enable the group to realize it.

Ultimately, the facilitator is concerned with enabling the group to arrive at the purpose for which it was set up, balancing the work and way in which it is carried out in the process of the group and helping it to progress through the stages of development, the issues around conflict and the implications of decisions.

Facilitator responsibilities

While the purpose and the process of learning groups are linked intimately, it is possible to separate out the implications of each, and in so doing, illuminate them further. For example, to manage the purpose of the learning group, the facilitator is responsible for the following, adapted from Hope and Timmel (1995):

- timekeeping;
- initiating discussion;
- setting out the agenda;
- asking for clarification;
- bringing information into the group;
- summarizing discussions;
- checking actual consensus.

In terms of the process of working towards the purpose of the learning, the responsibilities of the facilitator include the following:

- seeking contributions from all members of the group;
- encouraging participation from quiet people;
- preventing vocal people from dominating;
- setting the conditions for the group contract;
- expressing personal and group feelings;
- enabling members to resolve conflict and tension.

Roles in groups and effective behaviour

Facilitators may be able to perceive the activities of some group members as really positive, while others are quite detrimental. The following will help facilitators to analyse what it going on in the group and to facilitate helpful roles, while helping to alleviate negative influences through critical reflection.

Bradford (1978) identified a number of helpful and unhelpful roles, which I discuss in detail below, to encourage evaluation and reflection. There are many roles in groups which will help the group to progress and to meet their goals. Sometimes, the term 'role' is applied to the function of chairperson, secretary and treasurer but the groupwork roles in this context apply to the part people play in group dynamics rather than their function. While the titles of the roles are rather one-dimensional and simple, they point to a more complex behaviour pattern. To analyse one's own behaviour, it is useful to try to capture the complexity. That is, in some cases a member may be very encouraging while they may feel totally intimidated in another context. The following are simple descriptions of the roles.

Helpful roles

- **The initiator**, who gets things going.
- **The information seeker or giver**, who identifies the information needs and fulfils them.
- **The opinion seeker**, who clarifies values and suggestion.
- **The elaborator** draws out the meanings in the contributions.
- **The evaluator** helps to summarize and evaluate the work of the group.
- **The energizer** lifts the mood of the group and brings out better quality participation.
- **The encourager** brings out the best in the participants and the contributions.
- **The harmonizer** mediates the differences and helps to maintain a stable working environment.

- **The gate-keeper** attempts to keep communication channels open by bringing people in and stopping others from dominating.
- **The group-observer** keeps the group aware of its own process and progress.

Unhelpful roles

Again, these are simple titles which cover a complex phenomenon. It is important to evaluate your own behaviour, taking into account the complexity but never justifying harmful or hurtful behaviour. Ultimately, the objective of evaluation is to change unhelpful behaviour and to enhance helpful behaviour, for the well-being of group members.

- **The aggressor** works by deflating others and by dominating the group. This is achieved by talking too much, not listening and trying to control the group.
- **The blocker** takes up a position and stubbornly resists taking on other views or values.
- **The recognition-seeker** diverts the attention of the group towards him/herself, by boasting, acting in unusual ways or whatever.
- **The self-confessor** uses the opportunity of the group discussion to disclose personal details and to take the group away from its agenda.
- **The joker** diverts the attention of the group by play acting, joking, cynicism and so on.

Hope and Timmel (1995) add:

- **The arrogant person** who feels they are too good for the group;
- **The disinterested person** who is bored and disruptive;
- **The clique** who have a set agenda and who collude in secret or prearranged ways;
- **The whisperers** who form little sub-groups and speak quietly to one another when other people are talking;
- **The stubborn person** who will not be moved.

The facilitators have to look at themselves first, to reflect on their own way of being. This list is then useful to help to overcome problems in the group, to deal with impediments to their work. This may be helpful when facilitating conflict, and we will look at that in more detail in the next section.

Conflict facilitation

Activities and exercises in conflict facilitation are included in Chapter 9 (and more are available at this website: www.beyondintractability.org/index.jsp?nid=1).

When faced with conflict, facilitators need to have the attitude that it is developmental and can be very positive and progressive if they handle it with sensitivity. A number of steps are essential.

- diagnosing problems;
- initiating the approach or the confrontation in a way that does not demean the other person/group, and which does not take up a defensive position;
- listening actively to the other side, ensuring that all the issues are brought out and acknowledged;
- assertive communication in discussions;
- planning and generating solutions to the issues.

Facilitators must ensure that they remain just and fair, calm but prepared to confront and challenge the difficult issues and capable of facing anger and upset in any conflictual situation, while acknowledging their humanity and that mistakes can be made. The facilitator cannot take all the responsibility for conflict management. Various techniques are useful but every intervention needs good will on all sides.

The role of self-reflection and evaluation cannot be over-emphasized, and the following, adapted from Whetton *et al.* (1996), will help you to look at your own approach to conflict. In this model of conflict facilitation there are five responses to conflict: aggressive, avoiding, compromising, accommodating and collaborating.

Aggressive

This is the response where a person's own needs are met at the expense of others. This can be achieved through authority, manipulation, or just ignoring the other side. The issue then becomes a source of resentment and anger.

Avoiding

This response involves side-stepping the issue or postponing the facilitation of it. It stems from an inability to face up to conflict and the effects include frustration and perhaps the conflict arising in different guises or formats.

Comprising

This is an attempt to satisfy all parties by finding a solution that partially meets their needs. It enables a quick agreement and it may be ideal for some situations. However, it may be for expediency rather than to solve problems. Further, it may lead to manipulative strategies, such as overstating the issue in order to meet one's own needs.

Accommodating

This approach involves satisfying one set of needs and neglecting the others. It may stem from a desire to be friendly and accommodating. The value of the issues is not appraised at all and the use of this approach leads to a situation where one person or side is taken advantage of.

Collaborating

This is the attempt to fully address all the issues involved in the conflict. The facilitation of conflict using a collaborative approach entails seeking a solution that is satisfactory for everyone involved. It maintains that each position is equally important and ensures justice and fairness of the outcome.

Broadly speaking, the aggressive and collaborative approaches are attempts to satisfy your own concerns; avoiding and accommodating are attempts to satisfy the other person's/party's concerns; while the compromise is somewhere in the middle. Further, in terms of winning and losing, the collaborative approach is the only win-win resolution, when both parties gain, while the avoiding approach is a lose-lose situation, when neither party is satisfied, ultimately.

I-messages

The assertive approach involved in 'I-messages' helps with the expression of difficult issues without demeaning others. Of course it is no guarantee that the others involved will not be hurt, but acknowledge that.

Sometimes, when the group has progressed beyond early stages and is genuinely willing to come to terms with conflict, it is appropriate for the facilitator to allow a cathartic environment in the group, where members express their feelings about an issue. These feelings can be expressed constructively when the speaker uses the technique of 'I-messages'.

Examples are given in the section on assertive communication but it is worthwhile to explore them again in this context. The participant takes responsibility for the feeling which emerges in response to another's behaviour or issue. A negative statement, such as 'You make me really mad' is replaced by 'I feel very angry when . . .'. 'You are really thick . . .' is replaced by 'I feel undermined when you don't listen . . .'. 'I-messages' are extremely effective when feelings are running high. It allows the expression of feelings without diminishing the other person.

With this approach, the perspectives of the opposing views are stated in the 'I-message' way, and the facilitator enables the participants to discuss the issue, ensuring that respect is maintained. The discussion is terminated when the opponents agree to take the other's point of view into account. A full exercise on 'I-messages' is in the Resources, Chapter 9.

Finally, remember that gender, age, sexuality and race are other factors by which people are marginalized. It is vital for facilitators to understand that social relationships underpin the way people behave. Thus, a participant may defer to a perceived 'superior' or a woman may defer to a man. It is incumbent on the facilitator to recognize this and counter the effects as far as possible. The skills that underpin this aspect of conflict facilitation include calling attention to the effects in an assertive way and developing awareness around social relationships.

Conclusion

This chapter looked at the way facilitation has emerged and developed since the 1970s. Facilitation has developed alongside thinking on anti-authoritarianism and democracy in other spheres, especially the work place, but issues around power and powerlessness arise in the adult learning room as well as the work place.

The chapter examined ways of looking at facilitation, especially using Heron's work which is helpful in thinking about learning and teaching. An effective facilitator is empowering, not charismatic. Facilitators must reflect upon the provenance of knowledge in the content or subject matter of learning programmes when they engage with learning groups. However, facilitators must also reflect on their way of being in the group, congruent with the vision of adult learning for equality and fairness.

Reflection

Think about the best facilitator you have worked with. Look at their qualities in the light of the material in this chapter. Consider what you need to do in order to improve your qualities.

8 Innovative curriculum development

Key ideas: curriculum; syllabus; learning programmes; design; evaluation; assessment

Introduction

For me, 'curriculum' is a term that looks as if it belongs to formal education only, a mysterious part of the education system, with the possibility of a covert dimension, expressed as the 'hidden curriculum'. For adults, the language in formal education seems to be inadequate to express the different needs of adults learning. This chapter, then, will provide a short discussion on the meanings of the words 'curriculum' and 'syllabus', and their application to adult and community education.

Curriculum comes from the Latin for racecourse, with particular reference to chariot racing. This conjures the image of a track with clear boundaries, channelling the runners to the finish line. In the process of completing the race, the participants may have to overcome various obstacles, such as their own physical fitness, other competitors, the state of the track, any hurdles, twists and turns, but they inevitably head towards the finish line. The curriculum, therefore, is the totality of the learning experiences in any educational programme, in the progress to the goals and outcomes of the programme. In curriculum development for formal education, these hurdles include the societal norms, such as the expected levels of development for children, and the standards required for educational awards. But in adult education, the hurdles are quite dissimilar but equally challenging. The other word that is associated with curriculum is syllabus. Again, formal education seems to be the proper home for an idea like this, but just as curriculum is the term for the totality of the learning experience, for traditional students as well as for adult learning the syllabus describes in detail the specific content for specific courses. In this chapter, I will use the phrase 'designing an adult learning programme', interchangeably with curriculum and syllabus, and the intention is to help people to reflect on curriculum development, and equip adult educators to speak with authority on this quite neglected area in adult education and lifelong learning. Theorizing curriculum in adult learning is neglected because of the breadth of the field, which makes it difficult to subsume the diversity of the practice into a manageable, meaningful, neat theory. It is important though to think about this critically, without letting the qualities of the field slip away.

This chapter will continue with a close look at designing a learning course – curriculum development, and identifying the content – the syllabus. The chapter will then continue with a sample of adult learning curricula. It will finish with ways of assessing learning and evaluating courses. First, though, a short discussion on curriculum may help adult educators to reflect critically on their own programmes.

Whose curriculum is it anyway?

For formal education, the curriculum and the syllabus are intimately linked with the philosophy of education, the thinking about the ultimate questions about education, the why and what of education. The principles underpinning education are closely tied in with the values in society. For example, education was the key response at a time of very high unemployment in the 1980s, in Ireland, and, in the UK, there was a government department called 'The Department of Education and Employment' for many years. This shows the values that linked education to employment. In addition there are hidden agendas where the purpose of education is different from the stated one. Again, taking the example of education for employment, the hidden curriculum might have been to keep potential workers in education, in order to avoid the possibility of bigger numbers on the unemployment statistics. Thus, we have to see the purpose of education as both stated and implicit.

In terms of the set curriculum, the subject gets more complicated. Going back to the example of education for employment, if education was mainly to prepare students for employment, it would seem to be obvious that the curriculum would have a focus on employment skills. This would include training for specific jobs, as well as the general basic skills needed for literacy, numeracy and so on. However, the education curriculum is obviously broader than this, and it offers a much deeper education than simply employment orientations. Poetry, music, art and history, for example, enhance our lives immeasurably, even if we do not use them in employment. Accordingly, curriculum has the overt purpose of transmitting the knowledge that social policy thinks is appropriate to learners, in the way it thinks it is appropriate. And covertly, it transmits deeper values to learners such as those of art and music, on the positive side. On the less positive side, the hidden curriculum can transmit values on authority, status and control. Returning to our example on education for employment, the positive aspects of the curriculum revolve around the need for people's lives to be meaningful, pleasurable and fulfilling, as well as earning a living and being part of the community. However, the hidden curriculum can also be about teaching young people to accept the authority of the teacher, and to know their own place in the pecking order, to obey the authority and to accept the control exercised by the teacher quite passively. In addition, schooling is organized hierarchically and each layer of the hierarchy, from the principal to the students, must assert their power or lose it. In the world of the hidden curriculum, then, traditional students are prepared for the world of work by teaching them to suppress their lively, enquiring inclinations, to accept long working hours, to compete with others and to accept hierarchical organizational structures. This is a big debate in formal education. This debate can be framed in many ways, but primarily, when the curriculum is not learner-centred it is possible for it to fulfil the needs of society, the examination system, of teachers, or indeed, of the workplace, rather than the needs of the actual learners. It is worth mentioning this here in the context of adult learning, as an essential aim of adult education is to enable people to look critically at the dimensions of everything, including the hidden curriculum. However, while this discussion is very important, I want now to look at the art of curriculum development in adult education, bearing in mind that we guard against creating a hidden curriculum in the process.

The art of curriculum development for adults learning in groups

Designing an adult learning programme is a very creative process. Art and creativity are fully and uniquely human, and the process of working with adults rightly deserves a full application of innovation, ingenuity and imagination. There are a number of essential elements for designing a curriculum, and after these are incorporated, the more creative and engaging it is, the better it will be for the learners. The key elements include work that must be done prior to the entire process.

Identify the learners and their capacities

This entails an understanding of the different needs that adult learners have, including the fact that they may have been out of education for many years. They may be fearful and anxious or they may have social difficulties, including literacy problems. On the other hand, they may have a range of work experience, both paid and unpaid; they may have long experience of teamwork, in sporting and working environments; and they may have an array of skills that will contribute hugely to the group, for example, a brilliant grasp of grammar, poetry committed to memory or the ability to drawn and paint.

Review the field to discover the gaps you want to satisfy with the learning programme

Some of the gaps are obvious, such as ICT training, estate management and community development, while other gaps are more hidden, for example, the need to learn about the effects of drug misuse, or assertive communication. In any case, your work at this stage is to listen to the people on the ground, and observe what is current.

Identify what the learners need to learn in the programme

This is done by consulting with them directly, or talking with community workers, adult education officers and facilitators and so on. This element is more complicated, in that you may design a brilliant programme, but it must be flexible enough to change radically when you are actually working with the learning group. That is, the learners and others involved may identify a topic or subject area, but once in the programme, you discover that the learning needs are very different. Many coordinators recognize this so fundamentally that they consider the initial session as the 'foot in the door', that is, bringing the learners together, in the first place, and subsequently creating wider learning opportunities. For example, computer courses are often the way to connect with people in non-threatening ways, and once the learners are comfortable and relaxed, they can identify their needs for a myriad of courses, from creative writing to local history.

These elements are essential if the programme is to meet the needs of the learners. The preparatory work, in addition, is the beginning of the learning for the adult educators, which will continue during the entire process. However, sometimes organizers and coordinators have already completed this work and adult educators start at the next stage, planning in terms of the content and process of the programme:

- Decide on the aim of the course or programme;
- Decide on the outcomes;

- Identify the knowledge base that will underpin the course;
- Review the materials that will support the transmission of the knowledge;
- Identify the methods that are appropriate for the course that will suit the learners by empowering them, drawing on their experience and connecting with the content;
- Identify a range of processes that will enable the learners to review their learning;
- Identify the way in which you will evaluate the course or programme;
- Review the next stage, either a repeat of the same type of programme or fundamental change.

These elements are a guide to developing a curriculum, and provide a checklist to ensure that the interest of the learners is at the centre of the development.

Aims, objectives and outcomes

The first steps in any learning programme are to identify the aims and the anticipated outcomes. A good aim is very like target practice, in that you know where you are going. But it also contains an aspirational dimension, a hope that you have for the programme, linking if possible to the big picture. I recommend that instead of objectives you opt for the term 'outcomes', as this is much closer to the usage in learning programmes. These have evolved over the years, and now, instead of repetitive and wordy elements, the main way to set out the programme is to start with the aim and then isolate the outcomes. You then move on to content, methods, materials, timing, equipment and evaluation.

When you are trying to put words to an aim, think of it in terms of the ultimate goal of the learning. For example, the aim of this book is '*to explore the implications of learning in groups in order to shed light on the processes involved, to enhance our understanding of these processes and to enable us to use them for the benefit of learners*'. The aim is underpinned by the notion that we are agentic, that we can shape the future by our present actions and ethical principles.

On the other hand, the outcomes are much more concrete. For example, if this book was a learning programme, the outcomes might include:

At the end of this programme:

- you will be able to identity the main approaches to groupwork in adult education;

- you will have the opportunity to reflect on your own qualities as a facilitator;
- you will able to write an aim and the outcomes for an adult learning programme.

Words that are useful include: opportunity, write, practise, create, make, problem solve, and so on. Practise this by jotting down a few ideas, as they crystallize as you start putting words to your thoughts.

Knowledge base

The knowledge base for the curriculum in adult learning is almost impossible to contain. It depends on the topic and the particular aspect that you are taking. Needless to say, this should be your area of expertise, and you are the person who is in the prime position to identify the parameters. The key point to remember is to pitch the knowledge base at the level of ability of the learners. In other words, if people sign up for a course in social and human studies, it should be intelligible and understandable for them, neither too simple nor too difficult.

Methods

Adult and community education is probably the most creative and innovative arena for the development of methods of teaching and learning. This is because adult learners can give feedback immediately to the facilitator. In adult interrelationships, people have the right, and hopefully the opportunity, to question the issues of power and authority. In traditional learning environments, from pre-school to higher education, the educator learns how to educate from other educators. This obviously is not a closed circuit, but it does mean that the authority of the educators, albeit informed and earned authority, is upheld and reinforced. Adult and community education shifts that authority from the educator to the learner. Most crucially, though, learner-centred values ensure that the programme meets their needs, primarily, rather than the needs of the lecturers, programme directors, funders or institutions.

The learning environment is vital to ensure that the methods are conducive to adult learning. The space must be suitable for adult learners, including adaptable furniture with which the learner can form circles, small groups, creative props, and so on; adult information posters; catering facilities, for making tea and coffee and for celebrating; a welcoming, non-threatening atmosphere; access to resources such as books, leaflets and so on, and places to sit for small conversations.

When we speak about methods in adult and community education, we address the teaching/learning conundrum: does teaching result in learning? Is it possible that teaching can stand alone, without a learner, or does it always have to be in a dualistic relationship with the learner? Adult and community education problematizes this dualism, and asks very simple but telling questions about the dualistic relationship: who benefits from it? who is harmed by it? Adult and community education looks at the teaching/learning dualism and perceives that it perpetuates the assumption that learners, students and pupils lack knowledge, and the teachers, lecturers, tutors are not just expert in the knowledge, but also expert in what the learners need to know. Adult learning in groups adheres to the conviction that the role of the teacher is not to impart knowledge from an elite perspective, rather it is to facilitate the learning. Further, it is to remain open to learning from the learners as well as from continuous reflection and study. Otherwise, it remains in stasis, with an unassailable canon of knowledge. This necessarily has implications for the methods used in adult and community education. These methods are based on dialogue. This primarily stems from the belief that dialogue is the quintessential model for teaching and learning, based on mutuality and openness (Freire, 1972). In dialogue, people encounter one another. Dialogue fundamentally challenges the notion that one person in a teaching/learning duo is knowledgeable and the other is ignorant. Dialogue transforms the learners, enabling them to articulate their new knowledge. It transforms the educators, as they moderate their knowledge base with the new perspectives that have come from the learners, and through reflection.

Evaluation

Evaluation is one of those words that is co-opted by hotel chains and train companies to appear as if they are interested in changing their business from being profit-oriented to service-oriented, conflating the two as if they were interchangeable. Evaluation has also gone into the realm of numbers and statistics, and is often expressed in percentiles, for example, 60 per cent of guests were satisfied, while only 5 per cent were deliriously happy.

However, evaluation in adult learning groups is a much more profound endeavour, and aims to research, qualitatively rather than quantitatively, the opinions and values of the learners in order to improve the programme.

It is always useful to revisit the meanings of words, to ensure that they do not become empty vessels to convey what vested interests want them to convey. Evaluation comes from the French, meaning *'to find the value of'* (www.etymonline.com/index.php, 2008). 'To find the value of' is much more than seeing if something was OK: it enters the realm of judgement, opinion and merit. In adult learning groups, it necessarily encompasses the notion of improvement, as the intention of evaluations of learning programmes is to go beyond what went well. Evaluations build the experience of educators, particularly within reflective practice, but they also empower learners, equipping them to develop the capacity to challenge authority and assert their autonomy and interdependence. Evaluation opens the way to a more egalitarian, just and mutually beneficially adult learning programme.

Assessment

When we consider the assessment of the participants learning in adult education, we aim for more than a memory test or the regurgitation of our own notes. Assessments should give the adult learners the opportunity to engage with the topic, and should be considered as the continuity of the learning, rather than evidence of past learning. Self-appraisals are very empowering, and really help you as the facilitator to see what your programme has provided for the learners. Self-appraisals also assist with critical thinking.

Group projects are congruent with groupwork in adult learning. A piece of research carried out by a small group of three or four will have a longer lasting impact than a sit down examination. These can be practical, for example, organizing a small conference, or academic-ish, for example, interviewing people on a topic and writing it up.

Individual essays give the learners the opportunity to read and think. It is very helpful to invite the learners to create a title for their essay, but ensure that it has some element of reflection and evaluation.

Finally, learning journals are invaluable. You could leave time in your programme for writing, drawing or creating otherwise, the learning journal after each session, and the learner writes this up as an overall reflection. This has the effect of reinforcing the learning together with furthering it to new dimensions for the learner.

Designing learning programmes

Designing a learning programme is a rewarding, creative endeavour, which can reach out to participants in very tangible ways, but also in ways that can only be perceived, rather than measured. It also enables adult educators to work to their strengths, adopting methods that suit their personalities and styles, and 'joining up' the connections between the participants, the process and the content of the programme, the knowledge base, the providers and themselves. Designing a curriculum for adult learners is different to that for traditional students, with regards to the content as well as the learner needs. Adult education encompasses a wider set of subjects, from personal development to youth studies, and flower arranging to ICT for senior citizens. Adult classes are more likely to have a wider age range and different levels of prior education. On top of this, we have different levels of confidence and belief in all our attributes. This adds up to a very significant array of dimensions in any adult learning group.

Adult educators have to consider this when designing learning programmes. The positive aspect is that all of this diversity enriches and enhances the programmes. Therefore, instead of thinking of potential learners in a homogeneous way, it is much more beneficial to think of them as different and equal. For example, it is almost seductive to think of people by labels, like drug users, unemployed men, middle-aged women, working class, and so on, and to assume that they are all the same with the same needs.

To me, the starting point of designing a learning programme is the thought that adults are always free to leave, and the design must be interesting enough to keep them there, focused and engaged.

Summary

Innovative curriculum design and development is a dynamic concert of the views and perspectives of the learners, educators and accumulated wisdom from experience, evaluation and reflection. This chapter has explored the theoretical elements of designing a learning programme, including aims, outcomes, methods and evaluation. I now turn to the more practical aspects of learning programmes, with a sample design. The aim of this sample is to provide a concrete model, which you can use as a template for your own practice. This is not intended to be set in stone: rather, it ought to serve as a guideline that you can transgress.

Sample programme

Title: Introduction to Communication Skills

Overall vision

This programme aims to enable people to develop their skills of communication, in order that they enhance their capacity to relate to others assertively, respectfully, confidently and clearly.

Outcomes

At the end of this programme, the participants will have practised active listening and assertive communication. They will be aware of the values that underpin communication skills. They will be aware of the congruence between their body language and verbal communication. They will have explored the dimensions of communication in different contexts: interpersonal relationships, small groups, large groups.

Number of sessions: 10

1 Introduction to communication skills
2 Active listening
3 Assertive communication
4 Aggressive communication
5 Passive aggressive communication
6 Body language
7 Intrapersonal communication
8 Interpersonal communication: small group
9 Large group communication
10 Completion and summary

Methods

Mixture of methods, including:

- Input
- Dialogue and discussion
- Small groupwork
- Creative activities
- Role play
- Learning journaling

Session One: Introduction to communication skills

- Aim
  The aim of this session is to introduce the participants to the basic elements of communication skills, to provide the foundation for this course, enabling them to understand some of the dimensions of interpersonal communication.
- Outcomes
  At the end of this session, the participants will have explored the elements of communication skills, and will have practised active listening and non-verbal communication skills.
- Content
  Group introductions
  Input on the programme
  Basic explanation of the terms used on the programme
  Queries about the programme
  Introduction to active listening
  Introduction to nonverbal communication
- Methods

Name exercises	20 minutes
Short input	10 minutes
Questions and answers round	20 minutes
Role play on active listening	15 minutes
Role play on nonverbal communication	15 minutes
Self-appraisal	10 minutes

- Equipment/materials
  Programme guide
  Handout on active listening
  Handout on non-verbal communication
  Flip chart
- Appraisal of learning
  Self-appraisal by the learners, where they reflect on their own practice.
- Evaluation
  The facilitator asks the participants what they felt went well with the session.

* * *

As Jenny Rogers (2001) says, the first session is important, as first impressions have a lasting impact. Just as the facilitator has to welcome people, to be warm and friendly, the environment must be also. Thus, when you are planning the first session, ensure that you leave plenty of time for introductions so that people have a real opportunity to overcome their shyness, unease or discomfort. Even though you may have everything planned down to exact timing, you may need to let it go, in order that the needs of the group are met.

It is important to remember what *not* to do.

- Don't ask people to do anything that will humiliate them.
- Don't talk too much yourself.
- Don't ask questions of the whole group, and then assume there are no questions when no one asks. They may be daunted or fearful of speaking in the large groups.
- Don't comment in a judgemental way, in the large group.
- Don't ask people to write on the board or flip chart until you are sure that they have no literacy problems.
- Don't laugh at or ridicule anyone in the group.
- Don't interrupt them when they are speaking.
- Don't be too afraid ...

Remember, in designing a learning programme, ensure that you include activities and exercises that are energizing and fun.

Conclusion

This chapter explored the elements in designing a learning programme, and offered perspectives based on my experience of putting programmes together over the years. Most of all, I have learned what not to do, and this is still my key learning. The elements involved in programme design are quite mechanistic, but this should not detract from the excitement of working with adults.

Reflection

Design your dream course. Include the location for it, such as a beautiful beach or countryside. Design ten sessions, and write out the aims, content and so on. Think of who your participants might be. Think also, who might co-facilitate with you. Most of all think about the outcomes for the learners.

9 Critical practice: group activities and exercises for adult learners

Introduction

This chapter is composed of a selection of activities you can use with groups. As a method, activities perform many functions for adult learners. These resources will help to accomplish the work of the group. In addition, they will help the group members to develop their allegiance and commitment to one another. They can also help to develop attributes such as cooperation, mutual respect, tolerance and critical consciousness. And they can be a lot of fun – the lifeblood of group processes.

The activities developed in order to improve group processes, to enable members to work well together towards their goals. Huge encyclopaedias are available for human resource purposes, which I mention in the bibliography. For example, HR in the workplace often organize days away from the office, to play paintball or overcome obstacles in the wilderness to enhance teamwork. The essential feature of these games and exercises is that people rely on one another, thus highlighting the strengths of individual members and developing their trust in each other. They can be very enjoyable, and sometimes it is difficult to separate the benefits of the enjoyment of one another's company and the benefits of the game. These activities and exercises can be adapted for adult learners. Moreover, many of the activities were developed in adult and community education, in development education and so on, and many adult educators create their own. For example, for my gender studies programmes, I always start with the gender analysis of names, which also includes social and cultural analyses. This helps people to get to know one another, to think about identity, cultural and social contexts, and to gain insight into gendered expectations. That is a lot of learning in a simple activity. Activities have a crucial role in facilitating learning. In my experience of evaluating programmes and sessions, and as a participant in adult learning myself, participants will often highlight activities as being a source of deep learning for them, far more than the educator's inputs and 'chalk and talk' methods.

Pointers

There are a number of pointers to keep to the forefront when using activities and exercises.

The first is that of the capacity of the group members. I cannot stress how vital it is to tailor all activities for the group in question. Obviously, it is central to meet the group needs, but it is also crucial to match the activity with the style of the facilitator, the type of course and with a clear, transparent purpose. However, it is not always necessary to reveal the purpose until after the activity, if that is what is required.

When deciding on an activity, it is essential to consider the well-being of the group members. Take into account if there are literacy, cultural or gender issues, and related matters. In addition, take into account the physical capacity of the participants – pregnancy, ability, disability and so on. Be creative about ways of including people. For example, a wheelchair user could take the role of director if the exercise entails intricate footwork. However, it is vital to check this with the person concerned, as indeed it is for all activities in adult learning groups.

Take your own personality and background into account, and don't do any activity that you might be uncomfortable with. Adapt the samples below or repeat activities that you have taken part in previously.

Try to be alert to ideas that you could adapt for activities. You might see children's games or youth work activities that you could modify for use with adults. It is important to build up a menu of activities, so that you can keep your work fresh and vital, and pass on this vitality to your group members.

If you find that an activity is not going well, stop it and move on, unless you have a really good reason for persisting with it.

Ensure that the timing and activity is appropriate. Try not to take up a lot of time in a short session with introductory activities. This will leave the group feeling dissatisfied and you may not achieve the purpose or goal. On the other hand, it is worth spending more time on them as part of a longer programme, in order to attend to the foundation on which the group learning will depend.

Finally, and perhaps most important, alert the participants not to disclose anything that they do not want to. They do not need to feel pressured into revealing anything about their lives that is private and confidential.

The activities are categorized as follows:

- **Name exercises**, p. 121
- **Opening activities**, p. 125
- **Warm ups**, p. 130

- **Cool downs**, p. 135
- **Energizers**, p. 139
- **Cooperative exercises**, p. 141
- **Trust exercises**, p. 145
- **Values clarification exercises**, p. 148
- **Conflict facilitation activities**, p. 153
- **Closing activities**, p. 159

Name exercises

Name exercises aim to help people to get to know one another. In very large groups of 25 or more, this will take some time. At the beginning of a longish programme, this is very worthwhile, but if the time is short, with very little opportunity for individual participation or dialogue, a simple name round is better.

Breakfast roll call

Aim

To introduce and help people to remember the names.

Outcomes

At the end of this game, members will have introduced themselves in a fun way.

Process

The facilitator starts by introducing themselves and saying what they had for breakfast. Then, the next person repeats the name and breakfast and introduces themselves, adding what their breakfast was. This continues, with each person repeating the name and breakfast of each preceding member, and then adding their own name and breakfast. For example, the first person starts, 'I'm Bríd, and I had porridge for breakfast ...'. The next person says, 'That is Bríd, she had porridge for breakfast. I am Sonja, and I had pancakes and maple syrup for breakfast ...' This continues until the final person says the names and breakfasts of each person preceding and then hands back to the facilitator, who says everyone's name. The group members should help each other out, as the activity is not a competition and it will help people to build relationships if they assist one another.

The breakfasts can be a jokey, say, 'a fright', or 'a lie in', or exotic, 'champagne and grapes', or the actual breakfast.

Numbers   Fewer than 20

Time   20 minutes

Equipment   None

Pass the positives

Aim

To introduce people and reinforce their recollection of names.

Outcomes

At the end of this activity, people will have heard everyone's name, with a memorable tag.

Process

The facilitator starts the process by introducing themselves, and attaching a positive description to their name, starting with the same initial letter as the name. For example, 'My name is Michael, and I'm magnificent'. The next person says, this is 'Michael and he is magnificent. I'm Parminder, and I'm powerful'. The exercise continues until it arrives back at the facilitator, and they repeat all the names, getting help from the group members.

Numbers   Fewer than 20

Note: it is very important to get to know the names of group members, but when the group is more than 20–5, this is very difficult, and it takes a few sessions to embed the names in people's memories.

Time   20 minutes

Equipment   None

Unpacking names

Aim

To begin the process of gender and social analysis and to familiarize people with each other's names.

Outcomes

At the end of this session, group members will have reflected on the gender and social dimensions in personal identity.

Process

The facilitator explains that the round will focus on people's names and asks them to speak about what their name means to them and their families and communities, whether it has gender, religious, cultural and family dimensions. Group members then introduce themselves, assisted by the facilitator, who provides a social and gender analysis.

Numbers	Fewer than 20
Time	About 30 minutes
Equipment	A name book. Access to websites on the meaning of names will help, for example: www.behindthename.com/

Favourite things

Aim

To aid recollection of people's names, and to help the group to become more cohesive.

Outcomes

At the end of this session, people will have the experience of working in small groups and will be more familiar with people's names.

Process

The tutor asks the group members to form into pairs, and to talk about their favourite weather, pastime, food, colour, film, book, flower, tree, sport, clothes, holiday or anything that will get people talking. The pair then joins up with another to form a foursome, and the members will introduce the other person in their pair. Then the entire group re-assembles. Everyone takes a turn to introduce another person, speaking about their favourite thing.

Numbers   12–25. Uneven numbers can form trios and fives.

Time   5 minutes for pair work
              10 minutes for work in fours
              15 minutes for plenary

Note: Allow time for people to have a laugh, and perhaps introduce yourself with a jokey favourite thing.

Equipment   None

Scrunches

Aim

To help to reinforce the recollection of people's names, and to have a little fun.

Outcomes

At the end of this activity, people will know each other better, and they will start the process of enjoying the learning environment.

Process

The facilitator scrunches a sheet of paper into a ball and starts the process. He calls out someone's name, and throws the scrunched paper to them. That person repeats this, to another person, who throws it on to a further person. This proceeds until each person has had the scrunched paper and thrown it. The facilitator starts with a second scrunched paper, and the two scrunches are circulated. At the appropriate time, a third and maybe more are thrown in, until the entire process is chaotic and fun.

Numbers	12–25

Time	10 minutes

Equipment	Scrunched paper

Opening activities

Opening activities aim to start a programme or session, to focus people's attention on the topic and to help them to leave distractions behind.

Happy talk

Aim

To start the process of dialogue between group members in a comfortable way.

Outcomes

At the end of this activity, everyone will have spoken about themselves to the another, helping them to feel more at ease in the group.

Process

The tutor asks the group to form small groups of three and four. In these groups, they identify one reason that makes them happy to be in the learning group at this time. These reasons could include taking a break from a stressful working situation, learning something new, meeting with people in the group, knowing their children are happy, and so on. After the activity, the facilitator reconvenes the large group and begins the session.

Numbers	12–25

Time	10 minutes or so

Equipment	None

Shake, Rattle and Roll

Aim

To ground people in the present, helping the group members to leave any tensions and other issues outside of the session.

Outcomes

At the end of this activity, group members will feel refreshed, lightened, and ready to move into the session.

Process

The facilitator asks group members to stand in a circle. S/he asks them to focus quietly on the moment, standing firmly on the spot, take a deep breath in and out and look down to the floor or close their eyes. S/he asks them to relax, to relax their shoulders, arms, legs. They then open their eyes, and shake out their arms and shoulders, legs and hands. They are then asked to imagine that their trunks are hollow and filled with pebbles, and they have to rattle the pebbles. Finally, shaking and rattling, they are asked to roll their shoulders.

Numbers	No limits
Time	3 minutes or so
Equipment	None

Grounding principles

Note: Sometimes groups agree on a group contract, in which group members consent to abiding to a set of rules, such as time keeping, talking one person at a time, turn off mobile telephones, and so on. The group contract is subsequent to grounding principles, but it is generally more specific and primarily relates to behaviour.

Aim

To enable the participants to identify the principles that will underpin their group.

Outcomes

At the end of this activity, group members will have a list of guiding principles which underpin their work. They will have worked collaboratively to devise this list, and they will have reflected on the implications of their principles.

Process

The facilitator explains that the grounding principles are like a constitution for the group, in that they express their aspirations and values for the conduct of the group. The grounding principles guide the business of the group, and, like a constitution, the group can review the grounding principles if they are inadequate. These principles are drawn from a variety of sources, including the Universal Declaration of Human Rights, with the focus on tolerance, respect and freedom. In addition, principles from professional practice are important, such as active listening and confidentiality, when appropriate. Finally, principles from psychotherapy, groupwork, social work and community development include taking personal responsibility for our own behaviour, exposing hidden agendas, working cooperatively and commitment to other group members, the group purpose and the group process.

The group divides into smaller groups, and they list the important principles. Then, in the large group, the facilitator records the lists from the smaller groups, and collates them into themed areas, such as rights, behaviour, attitudes and so on.

The small groups reconsider this revised list, focusing on whether it accurately represents their dialogue.

Finally, in the large group the revisions are incorporated, and all group members commit to the principles.

Time	10 minutes introduction
	20 minutes small groupwork
	20 minutes large groupwork
	5 minutes revisions in small groups
	5 minutes final agreed list
Numbers	12–25
Equipment	Handout on sample grounding principles (see Appendix 1)

Group commitment

Aim

To establish an atmosphere of group participation with respect and mutual cooperation as founding principles.

Outcome

At the end of this session, the group participants will be moving further along the stages of group development and will have the experience of decision making and cooperation.

Process

The facilitator explains the reason why groupwork is used in education, training, community development, work and leisure. The group is divided into groups of threes and fours and the facilitator asks them to discuss:

- What conditions do I want and need to work in this group?
- What do I want from myself?
- What do I want and need from other members of the group?
- What do I want from the facilitator?

The facilitator notes these responses on a flip chart and endeavours to tidy them into a manageable number of commitments. These will be typed and distributed at the next opportunity (see Appendix 2). The facilitator assures the group members that they can revisit these conditions any time.

Numbers	12–25

Time	5 minutes introduction
	30 minutes small groupwork
	20 minutes flip chart work
	5 minutes debrief

Equipment	Pens and paper
	Flip chart and markers
	Typing facilities and photocopier

My space

Aim

To enable the participants to claim the space in which the session is taking place, and to help them to connect with every other participant.

Outcomes

At the end of this activity, participants will have met with everyone else in the group, and set up the room to suit themselves, as far as practicable.

Process

The facilitator asks the participants to clear the space in the middle of the floor, and to move randomly around the space. She leads the way, weaving in and out of people, watching out for any sign that people are beginning to move to a pattern. She then asks them to stop and line up according to their height. They resume their random walking. This is repeated four or five times, with lining up according to shoe size, colour of their clothes, birth dates, eye colour or any category that suits, as long as it does not have any implication of judgement, like weight, ability or power.

This activity can also be used to divide the group into small groups to ensure random membership.

Numbers   12–25

Time   10 minutes

Equipment   None

Reflections

Aim

To develop a sense of affinity between group participants and help them to work together without a sense that one is better than the other.

Outcomes

At the end of this activity, group members will have had some fun, they will have taken turns to be leader and follower, and will have developed a sense of trust.

Process

With the participants in pairs, the facilitator asks one person to make a gesture or facial expression and to move slowly and smoothly into more and more gestures. The facilitator can pick a theme connecting with the session. For example, if the topic is related to craft or economics, the gestures could be sewing, hammering, cutting for craft or counting money, using an ATM or such like for economics. The other person in the pair reflects this, copying the gestures and expressions. After a few minutes, the follower takes the leadership role, and the other person mirrors the new set of gestures.

Numbers   12–20

Time   5 minutes

Equipment   None

Warm ups

Warm ups occur at the beginning of the session or at a transition point of a session and they aim to help the group to build the energy for the session ahead.

Real listening

Aim

To help people to focus on what others are saying, and to reflect on their own listening habits.

Outcomes

The exercise will help to focus the participants. In addition, they will reflect on their listening skills.

Process

The tutor asks the participants to sit comfortably and, if possible, to close their eyes. She then asks them to listen quietly to all the sounds in the room, including sounds coming in from outside. They focus on breathing quietly and listening acutely. After a few moments, the tutor calls their attention back, and asks them what they have noticed.

Numbers   12–25

Time   3–5 minutes

Equipment   None

Active listening

Aim

To demonstrate the importance of listening in learning.

Outcome

The participants will have practised active listening, and reflected on how to apply it to their own work.

Process

The facilitator explains that active listening is a skill that is valued for developing relationships in learning groups, and ensuring that people's voices are represented accurately. This activity is in four stages: three stages of role exchanges and the fourth of feedback. The group divides into trios: speaker, listener and observer. The speaker recounts an experience which was significant for them, for example, meeting their in-laws for the first time, their first day in a new job. Again, alert the participants not to feel pressured into revealing anything they do not want to. The speaker recounts the event to the listener.

In the first stage, the listener is asked to avoid eye contact, look out of the window or down at the floor. They can nod and respond with mmms, the usual murmurs that occur in conversations, but cannot make eye contact or ask questions.

After three or four minutes, the activity moves to the second stage when the facilitator recalls the group to the task and asks them to swap roles. The speaker becomes the observer, the listener becomes the speaker and the observer becomes the listener. In this new formation, the facilitator asks the listener to maintain close eye contact with the speaker, but not to ask questions, nod, murmur, or otherwise respond, except through eye contact.

The third stage is the roles exchange again, with the listener asked to respond to the speaker with eye contact, nods and murmurs and questions.

Finally, in the fourth stage, each trio reflects on the experience, with special attention to the observers' and speakers' comments. The participants are asked to focus on their own experience of speaking with the different responses of the listeners.

Numbers	12–25
Time	20 minutes
Equipment	None

Tick tock

Aim

To focus people's minds and to have a little fun.

Outcomes

At the end of this activity, participants will re-focus on the session. In addition, they will have a break from the previous mood.

Process

The facilitator asks the students to sit in a complete circle, with no gaps or empty seats. The facilitator has two small objects, such as a marker, a pen, sticky tape, scrunched paper or anything that they can handle easily. They start the process by explaining that the objects they have in their hand are called a tick and a tock. They pass the tick to the next person, who asks: 'What is this?' The facilitator answers 'This is a tick'.

That person turns to the next person, who asks 'What is this?' The answer is 'This is a tick'. The tick continues about halfway around the group, when the facilitator introduces the same process on their other side, but with a tock. They look out for people who are not saying the full phrase and keep them on target. The exercise finishes when the tick and tock come back to the facilitator. The facilitator can also introduce a third object, a tack.

Numbers   12–25

Time   10 minutes or more

Equipment   Small objects

Drawing out

Aim

To help people to focus and listen, and to reflect on their own skills of communication.

Outcomes

At the end of this activity, participants will have been challenged to communicate accurately and to listen carefully.

Process

The participants line up their chairs in the middle of the floor, back to back. The facilitator explains that they are going to sit back to back, in pairs. One of each pair will draw a simple diagram or picture, and instruct their partner to copy the drawing by describing the details of the picture, not the title of the picture. For example, if they draw a house, they would give the following instructions: draw a rectangle, longer on the horizontal than the vertical. Inside the rectangle, draw two squares, at each end of the rectangle, with a small space between the edges of the rectangle, with a larger space in between. In that space between, draw another rectangle, this time longer vertically than horizontally, and so on. They do not mention the word 'house', but rely on their instructions.

After about five minutes, the roles are reversed. At the end of that stage of the process, participants reflect on their experience of listening, understanding, giving instructions and following instructions.

Numbers   12–25. Facilitator joins in if needed

Time   20 minutes

Equipment   Paper and pens

Complete the letter

Aim

To help participants to cooperate and ensure that everyone speaks.

Outcomes

At the end of this exercise, the group will have helped one another and had a little fun.

Process

The facilitator explains that this activity is a bit of fun. The large group divides into two or three smaller groups. The facilitator starts the process by nominating a theme for a letter, say, a letter to Santa, or an agony aunt letter or from a constituent to a politician. In a few minutes, each group has to complete the letter and read it out, collectively, to the large group.

Numbers   12–25

Time   15–20 minutes

Equipment   Paper and pens

Cool downs

Cool downs endeavour to help people to debrief from a session, and to vent any pent-up energy or feelings they may have.

Hot penning

Aim

To enable participants to overcome any reservations or blocks they may have about writing. It also helps them to make the most of learning journaling.

Outcomes

At the end of this exercise, the group members will have learned a skill that enables them to write quickly and without self-consciousness. People can apply this skill to any task involving writing.

Process

The facilitator explains that 'hot penning' is a skill which can be useful in all aspects of life, for example, creative writing, journaling, life story telling, reflection, academic writing and so on. The participants are asked to have paper and pens ready. The activity begins with a 'grounding' exercise. Then they begin writing, keeping their pens on the paper, forcing themselves to stay writing no matter what the writing is about, even 'I don't know what to write'. This is maintained for ten minutes.

The process of forcing oneself to write, helped by the group context, enables people to move beyond the blockage and tap into their own resources. At the end of the ten minutes, group members are invited to share their experiences. This exercise may not suit everyone, for example, people with literacy difficulties or those who are anxious about their capacity for writing.

Numbers   12–25

Time   13–15 minutes

Equipment   Paper and pens

Note: ensure that no literacy issues embarrass individuals in the group.

Tense and relax

Aim

To help participants to release energy after a session.

Outcomes

At the end of this activity, the participants will have discharged any pent-up emotions they may have following a session, and will have prepared to move on.

Process

The facilitator asks the participants to sit with their feet firmly on the ground and their hands resting on their knees. They make a fist, clench and release it, then the other hand, then, one at a time, the arms, shoulders, jaw, abdomen, buttocks, thighs, calves and feet, breathing steadily all the time. When they complete the tense/relax exercise they stand up, inhale deeply and slowly, and exhale strongly, quickly and fully. If there seems to be still pent-up energy, the process is repeated.

Numbers   12–25

Time   5 minutes

Equipment   None

Stretching

Aim

To help participants to reflect on their experience in session.

Outcomes

At the end of this activity, participants will have relaxed after a session and reflected on their learning, quickly and under slight pressure.

Process

The group have paper and pens ready beside their seats. If possible, the group could keep a learning journal, and this activity and variations on it could serve as a habitual exercise at the end of a session, to write or draw in the journal.

The facilitator asks the participants to stand in a circle, firmly grounded. They close their eyes, if appropriate, and image a silvery screen inside their eyelids. They stretch their arms over their heads, hand over hand on an imaginary silver thread. The facilitator then asks them to stretch their bodies, legs and feet, and to sit back in their seats. Then, they write for a few minutes in their learning journals.

Numbers	12–25
Time	1 minute stretching
	10 minutes writing or drawing
Equipment	Learning journals or paper and pens

Mix and matches

Aim

To enable participants to finish their dialogue in a reflective manner.

Outcomes

At the end of this exercise, the participants will have moved from their places and spoken to at least two others about the topic of the session. This has the effect of helping people to shift in their thinking as well as physically.

Process

The facilitator explains that this activity opens up the time and space to complete the dialogue that opened in the session. The participants are asked to think about the context, content and conversions in the session, and to identify two people they would like to engage further. They approach the first person and have a short dialogue and then seek out the second person. In the meantime, others will be seeking them out, so it is important to stay fluid and open.

Numbers   12–25

Time   10–15 minutes

Equipment   None

Making big pictures

Aim

To enable students to make the connections between a particular session and an overall vision or aspiration.

Outcomes

At the end of this activity, the students will have reflected on their learning, both the immediate session their recent adult education or life experience.

Process

The facilitator asks the students to think for a moment or two about their reactions to the session, linking it to anything else they have learned, or any book, TV or film, or any incidents in their lives. For example, if the session was on listening skills, they may connect this with their own experience of listening and the listening between Tony Soprano and his psychiatrist in *The Sopranos*. For another example, perhaps the session was on local history, and the students connect this with local landmarks in the area and films dealing with similar landmarks, such as big houses or castles, and the life people led in these contexts. The facilitator then asks them to write about this in their learning journals. Finally, they invite any of the students to share their reflections in the large group.

Numbers   12–25

Time   1 minute reflection
              10 minutes journaling
              1 minute final sharing

Equipment   Learning journal

Note: you can also use this exercise as a closing activity, when the participants view their learning with societal dimensions, such as poverty, class, development and so on.

Energizers

Energizers are designed to lift the mood of the group, especially if the members are tired. They are good for sessions immediately after lunch or late in the evening.

Music and dance chairs

Aim

To raise the energy level within the group and have fun to lighten the mood.

Outcomes

At the end of this activity, the group members will have moved around the room with energy and vitality, resulting in liveliness for the next session.

Process

This is like the children's game, musical chairs. The group arranges the chairs into a circle with the seats facing outwards, and with one fewer chair than the number of participants. The participants form a circle outside of the chairs. The exercise begins when the facilitator plays some lively music, suitable for the group. While the music is playing, the group members dance in time to the music. When the music stops, the group rush to sit on the chairs. The person who does not find a chair takes over the task of playing the music. They look for an opportunity to get a chair. The new person takes over the role of music player, again, grabbing a chair when able. The facilitator stops the exercise after five minutes or so, when people are feeling more energized.

Numbers   12–25, but ensure that there is enough space for the participants to dance.

Time   7–10 minutes

Equipment   Music and a music player

Islands and sharks

Aim

To raise the energy in the group and generate a sense of camaraderie and fun.

Outcomes

At the end of this activity, the group members will have moved around the room and they will have had close contact with and will have helped one another.

Process

The group participants clear the middle of the floor, moving chairs and equipment to the edges of the room. The facilitator spreads about four or five sheets of newspaper randomly on the floor with space between the sheets. She explains that these newspaper sheets are islands in a beautiful sea. Most of the time, the seas are very safe and wonderful to swim in, but occasionally sharks come close. The shark warning means that everyone has to find safe haven on the islands. The facilitator then directs the group members to 'swim', perhaps to try 'synchronized swimming', i.e. elaborate, fun, 'swimming' in trios and quartets. She then calls loudly, 'Shark Attack' and the participants scramble for the islands. After the first round, the facilitator removes one of the sheets and the group return to the 'swimming'. The process is repeated until only one sheet of paper is left, and the group is squeezed together, with people holding on to each other.

Numbers   12–25.

Note: If the group is very large, leave two or even three sheets, so that everyone can step onto one.

Time   15 minutes

Equipment   Old newspaper

Cooperative exercises

Cooperative exercises help people to develop a non-competitive way of working.

What am I?

Aim

To enable group members to identify the qualities of working in cooperation, and to reflect on their own cooperative qualities.

Outcomes

At the end of this activity, all the participants will have contributed to the discussion on the qualities that make up cooperative behaviour and work. They will also reflect on the particular quality they bring to the process, and the ways in which they could improve.

Process

At the beginning of this exercise, the tutor explains that cooperation is effective, efficient and economical in getting work completed. It is crucial in teamwork, and very important in group activity. Cooperation needs a supportive environment, with each person willing to listen to everyone else, be constructive and respond to others in a positive way. Cooperation relies on shared responsibility and clear notions about what each person contributes.

The group divides into smaller groups of fours and fives. They identify the qualities needed for cooperation, in terms of personalities, attitudes, styles and skills. They then identify qualities which undermine cooperation.

The large group reconvenes, and each small group gives feedback on their discussions. The facilitator records the key points on a flip chart, chalk or white board or computer and seeks agreement on a set of qualities.

Finally, each participant contributes to the learning journal on what qualities for and against cooperation they have, and identifies the areas for improvement.

Numbers   12–25

Time	10 minutes small groupwork
	10 minutes large groupwork
	10 minutes journaling

Equipment	Flip chart or board and writing tools
	Learning journal

Note: The qualities should include some of the following and the facilitator could include them if they are absent:

- positive attitude
- ability to take initiative without dominating
- ability to take a role willingly, like timekeeper or scribe
- knows and is committed to the task
- contributes own experience
- listens to others' experiences
- accepts the consensus
- recognizes the contribution of others
- ability to feedback assertively if others are dominating.

Team towers

Aim

To enable people to work cooperatively to accomplish a task, with everyone making an input into the decisions.

Outcomes

At the end of this activity, everyone will have participated in a team project, and the team will have to account on how each person contributes.

Process

The tutor explains that the task in this exercise is to build a tower with newspapers, using only sticky tape, in small groups. There will be a prize for the tallest tower provided that it can stand by itself for the duration of the exercise. The group divides into smaller groups of fours and fives and they take a pile of newspapers. The spend five minutes discussing how to build the tower and write down a plan. They build the tower and evaluate the process.

The tutor then facilitates the discussion on the 'helps' and 'hindrances' in the process. Group members then review the exercise in their journals.

Numbers	12–25

Time	1 minute input
	5 minutes discussion on building the tower
	20 minutes building the tower
	10 minutes plenary
	10 minutes journaling

Equipment	Old newspapers
	Sticky tape
	Learning journal

Complete the puzzle

Aim

To enable people to reflect on their own strengths and weaknesses in terms of cooperation, through an experiential activity.

Outcomes

At the end of this session, the participants will have completed a task which requires cooperation, and will have had the opportunity to reflect on their personal qualities.

Process

The facilitator prepares two or three reasonably simple crossword puzzles, dividing the clues into separate pieces of paper. The large group divides into two or three, each numbering six or seven. The facilitator gives a crossword grid to each group, and distributes the clues randomly among the different group members. Each group has to complete their crossword, knowing that the other groups may have some of the clues that apply to their group. The only rule is that no one can take a clue from anyone else, but anyone can give a clue to anyone or to any group. The facilitator sets the time limit, allowing enough time to make a good attempt at the crossword. When the time is up, the facilitator re-convenes the large group and asks them to reflect on the process, talking about what it was like to be in the group, how they felt about the other groups, and what they brought to the exercise. Focus especially on what helped the completion of the task.

Finally, they reflect on their learning in their journals.

Note: after an exercise like this, quite often participants have an uneasy feeling about their own or another's contribution. It is important to allow for a moment debrief before moving on, to allow the discharge of negative feelings. This could be a breathing exercise or a tense and relax activity, or an adapted closing activity.

Numbers	12–25

Time	1 minute set up
	15–20 minutes completing the crosswords
	15–20 minutes evaluation of the process
	10 minutes journaling
	1–2 minutes debrief

Equipment	Two or three medium difficulty crosswords adapted from puzzle books or created especially by the facilitator.

Trust exercises

Trust exercises help people to develop close connections with other group members, to enhance the working relationship and to facilitate affiliation to and bonding crucial to the group process. It is vital that the facilitator alerts the group members not to reveal anything about themselves that they do not want to.

Trust-building activities take careful handling in terms of the emotional impact on the group members. It is vital to ensure that the time to manage this is given to them if necessary, perhaps offsetting other plans for the session. However, it is worthwhile to devote this time to trust-building activities, in order to provide an authentic experience of group membership. Without a doubt, group learning is greatly enhanced when the group has built trust among the members, and this experience is transferable to all other groupwork situations.

Knowing me, knowing you …

Aim

To enable the participants to discover common ground with other group members and to reveal something of their own hopes and aspirations.

Outcomes

At the end of this activity, the participants will have spoken quite revealingly about themselves to another one or two people, and will be privy to others' hopes and dreams.

Process

The tutor explains that trust is an important part of growth and development, personal, community and social. This exercise is designed to help the group members to develop trust in one another, and to build on this trust for more challenging and transformative phases of the learning group.

Very importantly, the tutor also alerts the group members not to reveal anything about themselves that they do not want to. This is especially pertinent if one person reveals something particularly private.

The group then divides into pairs or threes. In that small group, they speak about some positive aspect of their lives not many people know. This could be anything: that they were top of their class one time, that their picture was in the paper as a bonny baby, that they won a short story or art competition, they bake great bread, can whistle a difficult tune, or once played for an elite football team. The other person expresses appreciation at the revelation and asks what it was like. After four or five minutes, they change roles, and the facilitator keeps a look out for the fair distribution of time.

Numbers	12–25
Time	10 minutes
Equipment	None

Every picture tells a story

Aim

To enable the participants to speak openly about their own stories, with the help of evocative pictures.

Outcomes

At the end of this activity, people will look at photographs, pictures, postcards and so on, and use these to access their own stories, while maintaining a certain distance, through the pictures, to ensure a safe environment.

Process

Prior to the session, the facilitator collects about thirty or forty pictures, including photographs, drawings, postcards and so on. These depict individuals, family groups, community groups, social situations, machines, abstract shapes, landscapes, cityscapes, flowers, plants, animals, indeed anything. Alternatively, there are photo packs available from suppliers for resources for adult educators and community development workers.

These pictures are strewn around the floor, and the participants select one or two that appeal to them. In the large group, they explain or describe what the picture(s) mean to them. The facilitator comments if appropriate, and allows a short round robin debrief.

Numbers   12–25

Time   20–30 minutes

Equipment   Collection of pictures

Show and tell

Aim

To enable people to speak about their deeper feelings, in a safe way, and to enable the group to appreciate the benefits of this deeper sharing.

Outcomes

At the end of this session, participants will have shared an appropriate depth of knowledge about themselves, and the group will have reflected on the meanings of this depth of participation.

Process

Prior to this activity, the facilitator asks the participants to bring in something that is precious to them. The examples of these precious objects include a journal, a lock of baby's hair, a perfume bottle from their teenage years, a football programme, a ticket to a concert, an heirloom, a garment, indeed anything.

The group divides into smaller groups of fours and fives. In these smaller groups, the participants show their precious item, saying why it means so much to them. After everyone has shared in the small group, the facilitator re-convenes the large group, and asks each person to reflect on the experience, focusing on just one person's contribution. Then, in the large group, they say what it meant to them to hear this small story, without identifying the person who shared it.

Finally, the facilitator finishes off the activity by showing and telling something of herself.

Numbers	12–25
Time	2 minutes, prior set-up, asking people to bring in items
	20 minutes in small groups
	20 minutes large group
	2 minutes facilitator's show and tell
Equipment	Items from the facilitator's and participants' personal lives

Values clarification

Values clarification aims to help the group to identify the guiding principles in their lives, and to reconcile these principles with the purpose and process of the learning group.

It is vital to take care of the well-being of the group members in exercises on values. Cultural and social mores, gender and ethnicity have a bearing on values, and it is important to establish rights-based principles in the group at the group-forming stage.

And the Oscar goes to ...

Aim

To help people to identify traits that they value in others, and to have a little fun.

Outcomes

At the end of this activity, the group participants will have examined values and qualities that they hold in high esteem, and will have shared their opinions on these values and qualities.

Process

The facilitator asks the group to formulate a list of qualities and principles that they value. She records this on a flip chart. For example, they may value work-life and home-life balance, honesty, democracy, active citizenship, loyalty, community development, family life and so on.

The group divides into fours or fives. Their task is to award an Oscar to the 'winning' principle, through discussion on which of these principles they hold in highest esteem. They can develop categories like 'The Oscar for Nurturing Youth' or 'The Oscar for Including Marginalized Men' and so on. They aim to get consensus on their 'winning' value, or at least a majority decision. At the end of their discussions, they come together in the large group. A spokesperson provides a summary of the discussions and announces their 'winners'. The facilitator sticks a star sticker beside the principles. Finally, the facilitator asks the group to think about the meanings of their principles and to reflect on their sense of other group members as a result of this exercise in their learning journals.

Numbers	12–25

Time	5 minutes initial brainstorm
	20 minutes small group discussion
	10 minutes feedback
	10 minutes reflection and journaling

Equipment   Flip chart
Learning journals
Star stickers for the principles list

Philanthropists

Aim

To enable people to dialogue about what is important to them, and to prioritize their choices in a fun way.

Outcomes

At the end of this exercise the participants will have discussed their values and preferences in the context of the priorities of other participants, and arrived at some common ground through consensus, ideally.

Process

The facilitator asks the group to divide into smaller groups of about six or seven. She then asks the participants to imagine that they are the committees of small social groups, for example, a ladies club, a youth club, an age action group, a creative writers group. A philanthropist has donated substantial sums of money to them. In their role as committee members, they have to decide how the money is spent. They have fifteen to twenty minutes. The facilitator asks them to reconvene, and to feedback from the small groups. Then the facilitator asks them to reflect on what kind of principles underpinned their choices. Finally, they are asked briefly to reappraise their decisions in the light of the discussion. The facilitator reviews these choices in the light of thinking about the aspirations for adult and community education in addressing inequality and unfairness, and the distribution of resources. A last round robin check will pick up any residual feelings of unease that participants might have arising from their own choices. Above all, the facilitator emphasizes that this a fun activity and is not to be taken too seriously.

Numbers   12–25

Time   5 minute set up
20 minutes in small groups

20 minutes plenary
10 minutes reappraisal

Equipment   *None*

Life largesse

Aim

To enable the participants to examine their values in the light of the decisions they make.

Outcomes

At the end of this session, the participants will reflect on their principles and review them in the light of others' principles.

Process

The tutor asks the participants to imagine that they are a community group, working with disadvantaged young people, including those who have alcohol and drug-related problems. A philanthropist saw that their lack of resources as a key obstacle to effective work and has invited them to apply for funds. Their proposal focuses on what they can do to redress the problems of disadvantage, prioritizing what is required.

For the purpose of this exercise, they need to identify the measures that are important for them, and to list them in order of preference, adding a rationale if it is not clear.

Next, they report to the philanthropist, played by the facilitator, who thanks them. She then recalls the group to the present, real time in order to discuss the items that emerge during the community group role play.

The facilitator asks them to think about the meanings of their decisions and to relate them to the values underpinning the learning group.

The activity ends with a final check-in, to manage any residual feelings of unease.

Numbers   12–25

Time   5 minutes set up
25–30 minutes discussion in the role play of the

community group
20 minutes plenary discussion
5 minutes debrief

Equipment   None

Desert island risks

Aim

To enable the participants to engage in clarifying their values, with some degree of fun.

Outcomes

At the end of this activity, the participants will have had a chance to make value-led decisions, and to reflect on the process and their choices.

Process

The facilitator introduces this activity by asking the participants to engage in a role play, and sets up the following scenario.

The group divides into smaller groups. Each of these small groups is composed of a teacher, a solicitor, a carpenter, a cook, a farmer, a doctor and an artist. They are on a desert island, but the resources on this island are very limited. They are expecting the rescue services but do not know when, and they do not have enough food or drinkable water for everyone. They must decide on the distribution of the limited resources. Someone can go for help on the sailboat, with provisions for two days, with the possibility of alerting the rescue services earlier, and four people can survive on the island for three days. Who should go on the sailboat? Who should get the limited resources on the island? Why? These decisions must be majority or unanimous agreement.

The group members then come out of the role play. They briefly report on their decisions.

The facilitator then leads the discussion on why they made their decisions: what did they base their criteria on?

The group do a final round, to manage any residual unease.

Note: this activity may bring up issues that impact on the group members' self-esteem, particularly is they have been disadvantaged educationally. It is important to rebuild confidence and assurance.

Numbers   12–25

Time   5 minutes set up
                20–5 minutes small groupwork
                20 minutes dialogue in the large group
                5 minutes closing

Equipment   None

Interim checking in

Aim

To help the group members to express their thoughts and feelings about their learning, halfway through the process.

Outcomes

At the end of this activity, the group members will have voiced any concerns they may have about their experience in the learning group, and the facilitator will have feedback on how the progress has been so far and if anything needs to be adjusted to keep the learning on track.

Process

The facilitator alerts the group that they have the opportunity to express their opinions about their experience of the learning group. She asks them to form smaller groups of fours and fives and to address the following:

- What is going well?
- What could be improved?
- What suggestions or recommendations could they make?

They discuss this, and create feedback from the small group, not identifying individual members with any particular point of the report. This is to ensure that no one person can be penalized if the report is not good.

The small groups reconvene, and reports to the large group. The facilitator checks out the recommendations and makes suggestions herself, drawing on her experience. Finally the group agree on any changes that might need to happen and the adult educator records these on a flip chart.

Numbers   12–25

Time   5 minutes introduction
             25 minutes small group discussion
             20 minutes large group discussion
             10 minutes final agreement

Equipment Flip chart

Conflict facilitation

Every group experiences conflict and it has positive and negative implications. The way the conflict is handled will determine if the conflict will help the group to make progress or will destroy their process. It is vital to allow sufficient time to deal with it and to define the problem as clearly as possible. It is crucial to deal with negative feelings in a healthy way and to help people to identify their part in the problem in very clear, concrete ways.

Conflict conversion

Aim

To enable the participants to manage conflict in a positive way and to ensure that conflict enhances the group process.

Outcomes

At the end of this activity, the participants will have had the space to acknowledge the conflict within the group, by identifying their experience of it. They will work together to transform it, and will re-embed it in the group process.

Process

There are three steps to this activity: AWE – acknowledge, work, enhance. The first step is to acknowledge the conflict. In any situation, people experience conflict differently, depending on the culture and personality of the person. Some people will feel the conflict very acutely, while others might see it as normal. The facilitator has primary responsibility, but the group has responsibility too. Successful facilitation will depend on the facilitator reminding the participants of the grounding principles of the group, revisiting them regularly in course of the learning programme.

The first step therefore, is to acknowledge and bring the conflict into the open, and to have each group member's expression of their experience of it.

The next step is to work on it. This entails individual commitment to transforming the conflict. This could be a written agreement, the redrafting of the grounding principles and/or verbal undertaking to work on resolving it. This step may look as if it is simply restating the obvious, but an aspect of conflict is quite often blaming others, with the expectation that the others must fix it. However, groupwork always looks at the dynamics of the interrelationships as part of the mix. Thus, together with the acknowledgement of this conflict, the commitment to work on it is a vital second step.

The third step is to use the conflict to advance the group process. The facilitator asks the group to divide into smaller groups, taking care to separate cliques or pairs, and asks them to come up with ideas to use this conflict to enhance the group. This entails looking at alternative viewpoints and evaluating them in terms of how useful they are to the group. For example, if the group conflict centres on a personality clash, they might decide to help the personalities to work away from one another. If it centres on ideological differences, the group might look at the guiding principles and see if both ideological positions are compatible with them. If not, the holders of the incompatible ideologies may have to reconsider their positions. If the problem centres on the tendency for a person or sub-group to dominate, those who dominate may not be aware of their impact on the group, and should commit to reforming their ways. If the problem is with the facilitator, the facilitator can modify their approach or justify it. The main issue is to use the opportunity to air the conflict and reduce defensive reactions.

This technique is very useful in group conflict.

Numbers   12–25

Time   1 hour or more
It is vital to allocate enough time for this activity

Equipment   None

Force field analysis

Note: This was developed by Kurt Lewin as a tool for analysing forces opposed to change. It rests on the premise that change is the result of a conflict between opposing forces, in order for it to take place, the driving forces must overcome the restraining forces.

Aim

To enable the participants to consider change in terms of the conflict between the driving forces for it, and the forces that prevent change.

Outcomes

At the end of this activity the participants will have considered if their conflict is resistance to change. If it is about change, they will have considered the forces for and against change and have settled on a course of action.

Process

The group acknowledge that they face a conflictual difficulty. The facilitator asks them to reflect if the difficulty centres on resistance to change, and to articulate the issues as they see them. Then, if it is about change, they identify the forces for change and the forces against change. These forces may include pressure from the outside of the group, like funders, accreditation criteria and community change. They may include pressures from inside the group, such as traditional versus radical values, younger versus older perspectives or ethnic clashes.

When the group identify these elements, the facilitator asks them to consider what would be the best for the group, their learning goal and their process. The group then divides into sub-groups to reflect on these new perspectives. Each group then feeds back to the large group, and the facilitator helps them to arrive at a decision, which they commit to.

Numbers   12–25

Time   5 minutes introduction
                15 minutes first round of consideration
                15 minutes second round of consideration
                20 minutes small groupwork
                20 minutes final round of consideration

Equipment   None

Assertive conflict communication

Note: Assertive communication focuses on communication styles that help people to articulate their thoughts and feelings in an open, honest and transparent way. It is useful for all aspects of interrelationships, but particularly in conflictual situations. See Handout (Appendix 3) for guidelines on the input.

Aim

To equip the participants with communication skills that can help them to deal with conflict, while keeping their sense of themselves intact.

Outcomes

At the end of this exercise, the participants will have a better understanding of assertive communication, they will have had an opportunity to practise assertive communication, and they will have reflected on its application to specific conflictual situations.

Process

The facilitator provides a brief input on assertive communication, based on the handout and their personal resources, if necessary.

The group divides into small groups of three and four, which look at the elements of assertive communication they need to acquire, if any.

In the large group, the facilitator uses the feedback from the small groups to identify the areas that the group needs to address. She then sets up short role plays to address these areas. Some group members may need to work on non-threatening body language, while others need to practise taking responsibility for their own emotions.

Next, the group divides into fours and fives, and looks at their conflictual situation, analysing it in terms of rights, confidence and body language. This entails asking the questions:

Are group members or outside elements infringing my rights?
Is the situation undermining my sense of myself?
Are people in the group threatening or imperilling others, either verbally or through body language?
Have the group any other appropriate questions?

When the participants complete this stage of the exercise, they reconvene. They feed back on their discussions, and ask the group as a whole to consider these elements. Finally, the group members commit to addressing these elements, with further meetings if necessary, or by modifying their own attitudes, beliefs or behaviours. This is entered in their learning journals.

Numbers   12–25

Time   10 minutes introduction to assertive communication
               20 minutes first round of small groupwork
               30 minutes plenary session and brief role plays
               20 minutes second round of small groupwork
               20 minutes final plenary
               10 minutes journaling

Equipment   Handout

'I-message' conflict facilitation

Aim

To enable people to take responsibility for their own feelings in any conflictual situation.

Note: 'I-message' process is part of the overall assertive communication repertoire. This exercise does not necessarily locate the cause of the conflict within any one person, but rather in a dynamic dysfunctional interrelationship especially one-to-one conflict. That is, it acknowledges that conflict can be due to oppression, the abuse of power, bullying and degradation, and it aims to empower people to take responsibility for their own reactions to these conditions. The analysis of the conflict then moves beyond blaming other individuals and towards a sustainable resolution.

Outcomes

At the end of this activity, the group participants or individuals express the genuine emotional and cognitive response to any given situation. This has the effect of shifting the tendency to blame another person for the situation, which helps to reduce defensiveness and self-justification.

Process

The facilitator acknowledges that a conflictual situation exists. They then explain that the way they want to deal with it is through the assertiveness technique of 'I-messages'. This entails that speakers identify the part of the situation that troubles them or affects them in some way. They think about that part, and express it, using I-messages. This means that the speaker starts their sentence with 'I think ...' or 'I feel ...', taking ownership of the thought or emotion.

For example, take a group situation where two group members clash over time keeping. Instead of saying: 'You make everyone wait for you because you are always late ...', the person says: 'I feel that I am not getting the respect I would like when you arrive late to class.' Alternatively, 'You're so intolerant when I am a few minutes late, you make me feel like a pariah.' In this case, the I-message is: 'I feel misunderstood when I am late. I find it difficult to explain that I am under pressure at home.'

Another example may be around a dominant person, one who speaks a lot, and does not always listen to others respectfully. Instead of an explosive: 'You're always talking, and you never listen' try 'I feel excluded when I don't get enough time to express my opinions, and intimidated when I try to raise it as a problem for me.' The alternative viewpoint may be: 'I feel shut out when I speak and then I feel that I talk more and more to try to overcome that feeling of exclusion.'

The group practises this for a few moments, with the facilitator calling randomly on people to express an imaginary issue in 'I-message' format. Then the group does a round robin feedback on the conflictual situation as they see it in the group.

The facilitator revisits the group contract, and reiterates the principles of respect, tolerance and dignity.

Numbers	12–25

Time	10 minutes input 10 minutes practice in the group 30 minutes or whatever is appropriate for the group process 10 minutes final debrief, revisiting the principles and contract

Equipment	None

Closing activities

Closing activities aim to make the transition from the session to normal daily activities. They help the group members to leave the session behind, including any difficulties they may have, and to move on. At the end of the programme, it helps people to bring the positive learning forward to the future and to leave negative issues in the past.

Mapping the journey

Aim

To enable the participants to engage with their learning using the metaphor of the learning journey. They map the learning journey in terms of the milestones along the way, the obstacles they overcame and the crossroads they passed, to reach their destination.

Outcomes

At the end of this exercise, the participants will have created a map that they will use as a metaphor for their learning. They will have described the landscape in their lives, with hills and valleys, rivers, trees, roads, estates, communities and so on, as metaphors for different aspects.

Process

The facilitator introduces the exercise, by explaining that they are using landscape as a metaphor for their learning journey. They will draw maps in a rudimentary way, describing what it was like to be in the learning group. They show the cardinal points of the compass, and some kind of land and/or sea. They will use this rough drawing in terms of the overall learning process, using the cardinal points to depict the overall direction, with key life events at the North, South, East and West points. The group members describe their learning using the metaphors.

For example, for the purpose of this exercise, the cardinal points may be 'personal development' in the North; 'Family' as the South point; 'Work' as the West point and 'Creativity' as the East point.

Next, they could draw a rocky island, with craggy edges, to depict pain and isolation, or a lush tropical island to depict relaxation and freedom from care. Alternatively, they may go for a boggy area, with a tiny railway crossing over, bringing the harvest to the outside world, which might depict a rich internal world with small conduits to others. The possibilities are endless, which is the advantage of the metaphor of landscape.

They then include in their maps various features, depicting obstacles and opportunities. These could include a raging river with a tiny footbridge, or a confusing spaghetti junction with no signposts, which they negotiate with their satellite navigation, or perhaps gridlocked traffic, which they escape from on a trusty fold-up motorbike. All of these images can convey a wealth of meanings that would be difficult to articulate in plain words.

They apply these to aspects of their learning journey. For example, the raging river may depict their inner turmoil, while the footbridge may be encouragement from a person in a small group; their spaghetti junction may refer to their first encounter with the group, or the confusion of new knowledge.

Finally, the group reconvenes and the members speak about their maps. The facilitator thanks everyone and closes off the session.

Numbers   12–25

Time   1–2 hours

Equipment   Drawing materials

Unwrapping the gift

Aim

To facilitate the participants in identifying their valuable learning experiences, even if it was in the midst of very difficult contexts.

Outcomes

At the end of this activity, the participants will have worked on uncovering valuable points of learning, which they take with them forever, while identifying the difficulties they encountered and leaving those behind them.

Process

The facilitator explains that every learning experience can have both positive and negative qualities, and some of the deepest learning comes from adversity. This activity aims to help people to come to terms with this.

The group image their learning as a series of gifts from the universe, wrapped in different types of packaging. These gifts may be tiny and the packaging huge. For example, the gift may be an insight into discrimination or the 'penny dropping' in a computer problem. However, the participant might have had to 'unwrap' their own beliefs, assumptions or prejudice before they get to the gift.

Either individually or in small groups, the participants write their gifts and their wrappings on separate pieces of paper. Then, in the large group, members can share with the group, if they wish. Finally, each person puts the gift into their bag or folder, and tears up the wrapping and places it in the bin.

Numbers   12–25

Time   30 minutes

Equipment   Paper and pens

Tree stories

Aim

To use the metaphor of the tree as a device for speaking about the growth and development that results from adult learning in groups.

Outcomes

At the end of this activity, the participants will have reflected on their learning in a holistic way, using the metaphor of a tree in terms of the roots, trunk and branches as stages and levels of learning, in order to situate it.

Process

The facilitator explains that the group is going to use a tree as a metaphor for their learning, growth and development.

First, individually they select a tree with which they have some affinity and which has meaning for them. For example, an oak is a very strong, big tree, and it grows from a small acorn. It provides huge shelter and food for lots of small animals. The timber is used for building ships and houses, barrels and furniture. The oak could be a metaphor for a basic skill like IT: powerful in itself, with lots of uses, from email for a loved one abroad to a learning journal. The participants might have stumbled across the information about the learning programme on a little flyer, and this small chance nurtured their interest.

They draw a tree and include features like roots, the kind of seed that it grew from, the bark and so on. They attach labels to any of these features that can symbolize the meanings in their learning development.

They divide into groups of threes and fours and speak about their tree stories. Finally, the large group reconvenes and the facilitator invites them to tell their stories, if they wish.

Numbers	12–25
Time	10 minutes introduction 20 minutes individual work 20 minutes small groupwork 10 minutes large group sharing
Equipment	Paper, pens, colours such as pastels or crayons

Mutual message

Aim

To pass on a positive idea to co-learners, and to massage each others shoulders in a fun way.

Outcomes

At the end of this activity, the participants will have reflected on things they have learned from their colleagues in the class, and will have given each other a shoulder massage to enhance their relationships and mutual appreciation of one another.

Process

The facilitator mixes the group members by asking them to line up according to a number of criteria, such as the colour of their eyes, the colour of their hair, their height, their birthdates, the initial letter of their names, their shoe sizes, the length of their hair, the colours of their clothes, or any quality that will not discriminate between them unfairly. As a variation, the facilitator could ask them to carry out the activity in silence, or with time pressures, or while singing, or anything that will increase the sense of fun and purposefulness. This should ensure a high degree of randomness, with smaller pairings or sub-groups dispersed.

The facilitator asks them to form into groups of three. Each person passes on a compliment to each of the two other group members, expressing appreciation for some learning point, discussion point, or any contribution they made to the well-being of the entire group.

Finally, they reconvene in the large group, in a closed circle, and stand close to one another, facing in one direction. People massage the shoulders of the person in front of them. After an interval, they turn around and repeat.

The facilitator calls time after another few moments.

Numbers   12–25

Time   5 minutes introduction
20 minutes small groupwork
5 minutes mutual massage

Equipment   None

Appendix 1

Handout: sample grounding principles

- We are committed to maintaining that the members of this group are worthy of respect and dignity, based on principles of social justice.
- Each member has the right to belong in the group, modelling an inclusive society, if s/he does not interfere with others' rights to belong.
- Each member has the right to freedom of speech and thought, provided it does not interfere with others' equal rights.
- We have the right to be different.
- We have the right to freedom of choice.
- We have the right to assert our own rights.
- We consider that we are responsible to and for one another.

Appendix 2

Handout: sample group contract

We will start and finish on time.

We will participate as much as possible.

We will deal with difficulties in an assertive manner.

We will listen to one another respectfully.

We will not engage in disruptive activity, such as whispering in pairs or making fun of any other participant.

We will let the facilitator know our needs, such as a cigarette break or a stretching break.

We will speak for ourselves only, keeping to 'I-messages', such as 'I believe ...' or 'I think ...' unless we have the agreement of the entire group to speak on its behalf.

If necessary, we will agree to confidentiality of the personal stories, discussions, decisions, or any other aspect of the groupwork which arise at from time to time.

We will leave the room in good condition, removing litter and replacing the chairs for use.

We will put our mobile phones on silent, or turn them off.

We will renegotiate this contract if necessary.

Appendix 3

Handout: assertive communication handout

What is assertive communication?

Communication that is open, honest and direct. It enables us to express opinion, feelings, values, attitudes and rights without impinging on those of others.

Why develop the skill of assertive communication?

It is important to develop this skill, in order to enhance our rights, to build self-confidence and to ensure that we are neither bullies nor doormats.

Assertive communication enhances our rights, reinforcing respect for others and ourselves. It helps us to recognize our freedom to control our own lives and to take responsibility for ourselves.

Assertive communication also helps our self-confidence by building a sense of security, acceptance and belief in ourselves. It helps us to understand that, while we are responsible for our actions, we do not control the wider environment.

Finally, negative hierarchical interrelationships produce bullies on one side of the relationship with passive or oppressed recipients on the other. Assertive communication overcomes this by respecting the rights of others, which prevails over bullying, and our own rights, which succeeds in countering passivity and oppression, in interrelationships.

What are the characteristics of assertive communication?

The characteristics of assertive communication reinforce the principles of rights, self-confidence and openness in interrelationships. This is conveyed through body language, especially. In Western societies, composed eye contact shows equality, trust and interest. Posture and voice should be peaceable and non-threatening, and on a par with the other person or people, not towering over them or shouting. Keep control over gestures like pointing, shrugging and gesticulations that dismiss or diminish the other person. Finally, the content of assertive communication again reinforces the message of rights and self-confidence.

What are the essential elements in the content of assertive communication?

It is essential to be specific rather than generalized. For example, instead of 'You always ...' you say 'This is the third time ...'. It is essential to listen to what the other person says, even if it is critical of you, acknowledging what they say but refusing to be put down. Finally, it is essential to take responsibility for yourself. For example, instead of 'You make me angry ...' you say 'I feel angry when ...'

Glossary

Adult education The practice of teaching and learning with adults, including night classes, training courses and skills courses. Adult education can take place in adult education centres, schools, the work place, museums, libraries, arts centres and so on. It is also called **adult learning.**

Adult learning The practice of education with adults, to highlight the experience, knowledge and reflection that adults bring to the learning environment.

Behaviourist approach An approach based on the idea that actions, thinking and feeling are observable behaviours, not evidence of an inner life or unconscious.

Community education The practice of education and learning with adults, with the focus on the learning needs of the community. It is usually organized and supported by the community, and it usually addresses social as well as personal needs.

Critical consciousness A moment of deep revelation, when we see a familiar experience, entity or action in a completely different way, a way that transforms our perception.

Curriculum A course or learning programme, including the content, methods and materials to deliver it.

Dialogue The practice of listening and speaking authentically, in order to hear others' stories, and to gain insight into our own.

Facilitation The practice of working with people in order to help them to achieve their purpose, in which the process is as important as the product. Adult educators facilitate learners by making the content and the methods congruent with their mature years and their intrinsic respect and worth.

Feminism The movement for women's rights in order to gain equality and justice in an unfair world. The slogan, 'The personal is political', captures the idea that we can interpret our experience in ways that tell us about society. Feminism is a model for other groups who are subject to injustice, for example, people with disabilities.

Group dynamics The interrelationships between people in groups. One result of dynamics is that the work they achieve together is more than they could achieve as individuals.

Groups Numbers of people gathered for a purpose. In adult learning, the purpose is their growth and development through learning.

Humanistic approach An approach based on the idea of human rights and how this underpins our interactions with others.

Integrative approach An approach that takes elements of all the other approaches, to suit the learning environment and learners.

Learning environment The space suitable for adult learners, including adaptable furniture, with which the learner can form circles, small groups, creative props and so on; adult information posters; catering facilities, for making tea and coffee, and for celebrating; a welcoming, non-threatening atmosphere; access to resources such as books, leaflets, and so on; and places to sit for small conversations.

Praxis The practice of working in adult learning that connects the learners with social activism. It combines dialogue, critical consciousness and the intentional purpose of changing the world.

Psychodynamic approach An approach based on the idea that our actions, beliefs and ways of being in the world are influenced by unconscious forces, which we need to uncover, in order to resolve them.

Syllabus A list of the contents of a course or programme.

Bibliography

AONTAS Women's Education Group (1991) *From the Personal to the Political: A Women's Education Workbook.* Dublin: AONTAS.

Apple, M. (1982) *Education and Power.* London: Routledge.

Benne, K.D. and Sheats, P. (1948) Functional roles of group members, *Journal of Social Issues*, 4: 41–9.

Bertcher, H.J. (1994) *Group Participation Techniques for Leaders and Members.* San Francisco, CA: Sage.

Beauvoir, Simone de ([1943] 1989) *The Second Sex.* New York: Vintage.

Bion, W. (1968) *Experiences in Groups: and Other Papers.* London: Tavistock Publications.

Blackmore, S. (2005) *Consciousness: A Very Short Introduction.* Oxford: Oxford University Press.

Bradford, L.P. (1976) *Making Meetings Work: A Guide for Leaders and Group Members.* La Jolla, CA: University Associates Press.

Brookfield, S. (1990) *The Skillful Teacher: On Technique, Trust, and Responsiveness in the Classroom.* San Francisco, CA: Jossey-Bass Publishers.

Bourdieu, P. (1984) *Distinctions: A Social Critique of the Judgement of Taste.* Cambridge, MA: Harvard University Press.

Bourdieu, P. (1983) Forms of capital, J.C. Richards (ed.) *Handbook of Theory and Research for the Sociology of Education.* New York: Greenwood Press.

Bourdieu, P. (1977) *Outline of a Theory of Practice.* Cambridge: Cambridge University Press.

Buber, M. (1973) *Meetings*, trans. M. Friedman. La Salle, IL: Open Court Publishing.

Butler, S. and Wintram, C. (1991) *Feminist Groupwork.* London: Sage.

Carr, W. and Kemmis, S. (1986) *Becoming Critical: Education, Knowledge, and Action Research.* Lewes: Falmer.

Classics in the History of Psychology, http://psychclassics.yorku.ca/Sherif/index.htm (accessed 31 March 2008).

Commission of the European Communities (2005) *Communication from the Commission, Mobilising the Brainpower of Europe: Enabling Universities to Make their Full Contribution to the Lisbon Strategy.* Brussels: COM.

Commission of the European Communities (2000) *A Memorandum on Lifelong Learning.* Brussels: COM.

Connolly, B. (2007) Beyond the Third Way: new challenges for adult and community education, in B. Connolly, T. Fleming, D. McCormack and A. Ryan (eds) *Radical Learning for Liberation*. Maynooth: MACE.

Connolly, B. (2005) Learning from the women's community education movement in Ireland, in J. Crowther, V. Galloway, and I. Martin, (eds) *Popular Education: Engaging the Academy*. Leicester: NIACE.

Connolly, B. (2003) Women's community education: listening to the voices, *The Adult Learner, Journal of Adult Education in Ireland*. AONTAS, Dublin: 9–19.

Connolly, B. (1999) Groupwork and facilitation: a feminist evaluation of their role in transformative adult and community education, in B. Connolly and A.B. Ryan (eds) *Women and Education in Ireland*. Maynooth: MACE.

Coover, V., Deacon, E., Esser, C. and Moore, C. (1981) *Resource Manual for a Living Revolution*. Philadelphia: New Society Publishers.

Coyle, G.L. (1947) *Group Experience and Democratic Values*. New York: Women's Press.

Crowther, J., Martin, I. and Shaw, M. (eds) (1999) *Popular Education and Social Movements in Scotland Today*. Leicester: NIACE.

Dewey, J. (1970) *John Dewey,* edited with an introduction by M. Skilbeck. London: Collier-McMillan.

Dewey, J. (1925) *Nature and Experience*. Chicago: Open Court Publishing.

Encyclopaedia of Psychology (2008) www.enotes.com/gale-psychology-encyclopedia/defense-mechanisms (accessed 31 March 2008).

Field, J. (2005) *Social Capital and Lifelong Learning*. Bristol: Policy Press.

Field, J. (2001) Lifelong education, *International Journal of Lifelong Education*, 20(1–2): 3–15.

Field, J. (2000) *Lifelong Learning and the New Educational Order*. Stoke on Trent: Trentham Books.

Foley, G. (2004) Introduction: the state of adult education and learning, in G. Foley (ed.) *Dimensions of Adult Learning: Adult Education and Training in a Global Era*. Maidenhead: Open University Press.

Freire, P. (2008) http://freire.education.mcgill.ca/node/37 (accessed 31 March 2008).

Freire, P. (1972) *The Pedagogy of the Oppressed*. Harmondsworth: Penguin.

Freud, S. (1923) The Ego and the Id, in *The Complete Psychological Works of Sigmund Freud* (1953). London: Hogarth Press.

Freud, A. (1974) *Introduction to Psychoanalysis: Lectures for Child Analysts and Teachers, 1922–1935*. London: Hogarth Press.

Giddens, A. (1994) *Beyond Left and Right – The Future of Radical Politics*. Cambridge: Polity Press.

Giddens, A. (1986) *Sociology: A Brief but Critical Introduction*. London: Macmillan Education.

Gilligan, C. (1993) *In a Different Voice. Psychological Theory and Women's Development*. Cambridge, MA: Harvard University Press.

Giroux, H. (2005) *What is Critical Pedagogy?* www.perfectfit.org/CT/giroux1.html (accessed 31 March 2008).

Giroux, H. (1992) *Border Crossings*. Boston: Routledge & Kegan Paul.

Glassman, U. and Kates, L. (1990) *Group Work: A Humanistic Approach*. Newbury Park, CA: Sage.

Government of Ireland (2000) *Learning for Life: White Paper on Adult Education*. Dublin: Government Publications.

Gramsci, A. (1971) *Selection from Prison Notebooks*. London: Lawrence and Wishart.

Habermas, J. (1987) Life-forms, morality and the task of the philosopher, in P. Dews, (ed.) *Autonomy and Solidarity – Interviews with Jurgen Habermas*. London: Verso.

Heron, J. (1990) *Helping the Client: A Creative Practical Guide*. London: Sage.

Hodes, A. (1972) *Encounter with Martin Buber*. London: Allen Lane/Penguin.

Hogan, C. (2002) *Understanding Facilitation: Theory and Principles*. London: Kogan Page.

Hope, A. and Timmel, S. (1995) *Training for Transformation*. Zimbabwe: Mambo Press.

hooks, bell (2008) www.allaboutbell.com/ (accessed 31 March 2008).

hooks, bell (2008) www.com.washington.edu/Program/publicscholarship/ps_marwick.pdf (accessed 31 March 2008).

hooks, bell (1994) *Education as Freedom*. New York: Routledge.

Jarvis, P. (2006) *Towards a Comprehensive Theory of Human Learning*. London: Routledge.

Jaques, D. (2000) *Learning in Groups*. London: Croom Helm.

Kanpol, B. (1999) *Critical Pedagogy: An Introduction*, 2nd edn. London: Bergin & Garvey.

Kett, J.F. (1994) *The Pursuit of Knowledge Under Difficulties. From Self-Improvement to Adult Education in America, 1750–1990*. Stanford, CA: Stanford University Press.

King, P., O'Driscoll, S. and Holden, S. (2003) *Gender and Learning*. Dublin: AONTAS.

Konopka, G. (1962) *Social Group Work: A Helping Process*. Englewood Cliffs, NT: Prentice Hall.

Kristeva, J. (1986) *The Kristeva Reader*, edited by Toril Moi. Oxford: Blackwell.

Lather, P. (1991) *Getting Smart: Feminist Research and Pedagogy With/in the Postmodern*. London: Routledge.

Lederman, W. (1976) *Introduction to Group Theory*. London: Longman.

Lewin, K. (1948) *Resolving Social Conflicts; Selected Papers on Group Dynamics*. New York: Harper & Row.

Lindeman, E.C. (1926) *The Meaning of Adult Education*. New York: New Republic.

Lindenfield, G. (1986) *Assert Yourself: A Self-help Assertiveness Programme for Men and Women*. London: Thorsons.

Longworth, N. (2003) *Lifelong Learning in Action: Transforming Education in 21st Century*. London: Routledge.

Luft, J. (1984) *Processes: An Introduction to Group Dynamics*. Palo Alto, CA: Mayfield.

Luke, C. and Gore, J. (eds) (1992) *Feminisms and Critical Pedagogy*. London: Routledge.

Lukes, S. (2005) *Power: A Radical View*, 2nd edn. London: Macmillan Palgrave.

Lynch, K. and Lodge, A. (2002) *Equality and Power in Schools*. London: Routledge/Falmer.

Lynch, K. (1999) *Equality in Education*. Dublin: Gill and Macmillan.

Lynch, K. (1989) *The Hidden Curriculum: Reproduction in Education, A Reappraisal*. London: The Falmer Press.

McLaren, P. (1989) *Life in Schools*. New York: Longman.

Madoo Lengermann, P. and Niebrugge-Brantley, J. (2003) Contemporary Feminist Theory, in G. Ritzer, and D.J. Goodman, *Sociological Theory*, 6th edn. New York: McGrawHill.

Maslow, A.H. (1943) *A Theory of Human Motivation*, first published in the Psychological Review, 50, 370–396, and available at: http://psych classics.yorku.ca/Maslow/motivation.htm: (accessed 31 March 2008).

Mezirow, J. and associates (2000) *Learning as Transformation: Critical Perspectives on a Theory in Progress*. San Francisco: Jossey Bass.

Moore, A.B. and Feldt, J.A. (1992) *Facilitating Community and Decision-making Groups*. Melbourne, FL: Kreiger.

Mulligan, J. (1993) *The Personal Management Handbook*. London: Warner Books.

Newman, M. (2006) *Teaching Defiance: Stories and Strategies for Activist Educators*. San Francisco, CA: Jossey-Bass.

OECD (Organization for Economic Co-operation and Development) (1996) 'Literacy Skills for the Knowledge Society, *International Adult Literacy Survey*. Paris: OECD.

OECD (Organization for Economic Co-operation and Development) (2003) *The Role of National Qualifications Systems in Promoting Lifelong Learning*. Paris: OECD.

OECD (Organisation for Economic Co-operation and Development) (2004) *Policy Brief: Lifelong Learning*. Paris: OECD.

Owens, T. (2000) *Men on the Move: A Study of Barriers to Male Participation in Education and Training Initiatives*. Dublin: AONTAS.

Palmer, P.J. (1998) *The Courage to Teach: Exploring the Inner Landscape of the Teacher's Life*. San Francisco, CA: Jossey-Boss.

Powell, F. and Geoghegan, M. (2004) *The Politics of Community Development: Reclaiming Civil Society or Reinventing Governance?* Dublin: A&A Farmer.

Prendiville, P. (2007) *Developing Facilitation Skills*. Dublin: CPA.

Reid, K.E. (1981) Formulation of a method, 1920–1936, in *From Character Building to Social Treatment. The History of the Use of Groups in Social Work*. Westport, CT.

Ritzer, G. and Goodman, D.J. (2003) *Sociological Theory*, 6th edn. New York: McGraw-Hill.

Ritzer, G. (1981) *Towards an Integrated Sociological Paradigm: The Search for an Exemplar and an Image of the Subject Matter*. Boston: Allyn and Bacon.

Rogers, C. (1980) *A Way of Being*. Boston, MA: Houghton Mifflin.

Rogers, C. (1983) *Freedom to Learn for the 1980s*. Columbus, OH: Merrill.

Rogers, C., (1951) *Client-centred Therapy: its Current Practice, Implications and Theory*. London: Constable.

Rogers, J. (2000) *Adult Learning*, 4th edn. Maidenhead: Open University Press.

Ryan, A.B. (2001) *Feminist Ways of Knowing: Towards Theorising the Person for Radical Adult Education*. Leicester: NIACE.

Ryan, A.B. and Connolly, B. (2000) Women's Community Education in Ireland: the need for new directions towards 'really useful knowledge' in J. Thompson (ed.) *Engaging the Academy, The Politics and Practice of Widening Participation in Higher Education*. Leicester: NIACE.

Sartre, J.P. (1989) *Being and Nothingness: An Essay on Phenomenological Ontology*. London: Routledge.

Schellenburg, J.A. (1978) *Masters of Social Psychology*. Oxford: Oxford University Press.

Schneider Corey, M. and Corey, G. (2002) *Groups: Process and Practice*, 6th edn. Pacific Grove, CA: Brooks/Cole.

Seligman, M. (2004) *Authentic Happiness: Using the New Positive Psychology to Realize your Potential for Lasting Fulfilment*. New York: Free Press.

Senge, P. (1999) *The Dance of Change: The Challenges of Sustaining Momentum in Learning Organisation*. London: Nicholas Brealey.

Senge, P. (2006) *The Fifth Discipline – The Art and Practice of the Learning Organisation*. New York: Doubleday Currency.

Sharif, M, Harvey, O.J., White, B.J., Hood, W.R., and Sherif, C. (1988) *The Robbers Cave Experiment: Intergroup Conflict and Cooperation*. Middleton, CT: Wesleyan University Press.

Skinner, B.F. (2006) *About Behaviourism.* London: Plimico.

Slater, L. (2004) *Opening Skinner's Box: Great Psychological Experiments of the Twentieth Century.* London: Bloomsbury.

Smith, M.K. (2002) Jerome S. Bruner and the Process of Education', *The Encyclopedia of Informal Education.* www.infed.org/thinkers/bruner.htm (accessed 31 March 2008).

Sugrue, C. (ed.) (2004) *Curriculum and Ideology: Irish Experiences, International Perspectives.* Dublin: Liffey Press.

Tennant, M. (1997) *Psychology and Adult Learning.* London: Routledge.

Tight, M. (2002) *Key Concepts in Adult Learning and Training,* 2nd edn. London: Routledge.

Tonnies, F. (1963) *Community & Society (Gemeinschaft und Gesellschaft).* New York: Harper and Row.

Thompson, J. (1996) 'Really Useful Knowledge': linking theory to practice, in B. Connolly, T. Fleming, D. McCormack, and A. Ryan (eds) *Radical Learning for Liberation.* Maynooth: MACE.

Tovey, H. and Share, P. (2003) *A Sociology of Ireland,* 2nd edn. Dublin: Gill and Macmillan.

Tuckman, B. (1965) Developmental sequence in small groups, *Psychological Bulletin,* 63: 384–99 dennislearningcenter.osu.edu/references/GROUP%20DEV%20ARTICLE.doc. (accessed 31 March 2008).

Tyson, T. (1998) *Working with Groups,* 2nd edn. South Yarra: Macmillan Education Australia.

WEA (2008) www.wea.org.uk/aboutus/ (accessed 31 March 2008).

Weedon, C. (1997) *Feminist Practice and Poststructuralist Theory,* 2nd edn. Oxford: Blackwell.

Weiner, G. (1994) *Feminisms in Education: An Introduction.* Buckingham: Open University Press.

WERRC (2003) *A Whole New World: A Feminist Model of Community and Lifelong Learning.* Dublin: WERRC.

WERRC (2001) *At the Forefront: The Role of Women's Community Education in Combating Poverty and Disadvantage in the Republic of Ireland.* Dublin: AONTAS and WERRC.

West, L. (2006) *Back to the Future.* www.canterbury.ac.uk/education/departments/educational-research/centres/international-studies-of-participation-and-diversity/research/Back-to-the-future-adults-learning[1].pdf (accessed 31 March 2008).

Whetten, D., Cameron, K. and Woods, M. (1996) *Effective Conflict Management.* London: HarperCollins.

Williamson, B. (1998) *Lifeworlds and Learning: Essays in the Theory, Philosophy and Practice of Lifelong Learning.* Leicester: NIACE.

Yeaxlee, B.A. (1929) *Lifelong Education: A Sketch of the Range and Significance of the Adult Education Movement.* London: Cassell.

Index